For
Evelyn

In appreciation for
your Christian Service

[signature]

10-10-83

DAYBREAK: FAITH FOR ORDINARY DAYS

JAMES M. PORCH

BROADMAN PRESS
Nashville, Tennessee

© Copyright 1983 • Broadman Press.

All rights reserved.

4252-06

ISBN: 0-8054-5206-0

Dewey Decimal Classification: 248.4

Subject Heading: CHRISTIAN LIFE

Library of Congress Catalog Card Number: 82-82951

Printed in the United States of America

For

Lynn, Scott, and Terri.

Each daybreak with you is a fresh adventure in living.

In Appreciation

. . . to the First Baptist Church of Tullahoma, Tennessee. You listened to these arrangements of ideas, tales, stories, and commentaries—all intended to grapple with life and grace. Some of you encouraged me to write them down. This offering is my response to your affirmation.

. . . to Tim Hendrickson, friend, helpful critic, and Christian gentleman. Thanks for reading the chapters and catching a variety of errors.

. . . to Jean Halcomb, pastor's secretary and Christian lady possessing a cooperative spirit and genuine dedication to the Christian ministry. Thank you for typing and retyping.

. . . to the three Porches—Lynn, Scott, and Terri—for gracing me with quiet hours in the garage study as I struggled to meet a short deadline.

Contents

Foreword

If I am to cope day by day with life, I must accept personal reality about myself and receive God's grace.

Perception of reality is not necessarily automatic. I must perennially walk on through life and watch out for signs—DANGER, ILLUSION AHEAD. Personal reality is discovered as I consciously endeavor to keep in touch with myself and give personal assent and affirmation to the truth I discover about myself. Once self-truth is accepted I become ready to receive God's grace. Thus accepted, self-truth becomes blessed by the gift of divine grace. In other words, to possess "the strength not to faint" I must be willing to admit the truth about myself, welcome the grace of God, and honestly and humanly affirm, "I am what I am by the grace of God."

These chapters are my attempt to assess the validity of this thesis: Faith for ordinary days requires accepting personal reality and receiving God's grace.

I
Accepting Personal Reality

1
My Escape Ships Keep Sailing from Joppa

"Hang in there!"

That often-heard and well-intended "slogan of encouragement" is not always well received. We do not possess the constant natural desire to welcome illness, death, unplanned expense, additional work, or a thousand other threatening interruptions. Inevitably, within the storm of some stressful circumstance we each wish someone would say "It's OK to run away."

Consider Jonah.

The old missionary prophet represents a recurring tendency to escape from God and life. True, a great fish was used to rescue a rebellious preacher nursing a sour attitude, and God still delivered his call of repentance to Nineveh. However, a message about escapism, an often attractive and convenient ploy, available to all of us, is the real warning of the book. When Jonah traveled to Joppa, intending to board a ship for Tarshish, he was exercising the choice of escapism, his personal liberty to run away, even to attempt to flee from God.

In modern life, our ships are always waiting "to sail from Joppa." These vessels are symbolized in the myriad of temptations to run away rather than face the realities of life. No one always refuses to run away. We do run. We have run away. We will run again. All of us harbor a personal running point, that potential crisis moment when we feel we have exhausted our ability to cope. The tragedy, though, arrives when fleeing or running away becomes a life-style. Too often today morally upright and well-intentioned persons become chained to the choice to flee, and they constantly seek passage on a ship out of

Joppa to carry them away from the unwelcome threats, events, and circumstances of life. Repeated trips on such ships are simultaneously dangerous en route and destined for ultimate disaster.

Escape: A Persistent Temptation

Beware!

A Jonah-like trait is always present in each of us. The tendency to run away on Joppa ships is sometimes disguised but still real. A fifth grader is consistently tardy. An employee works in perpetual conflict, in rebellion with his job description. The parent in mid-life crisis chooses divorce, or, more drastically, abandons his family. Add disease and pain, a radically changing world, the economic stress of inflation, the threat of nuclear accident or holocaust and death, and the conclusion is easy—the scope of the affliction of escapism is wide and widening. Somewhere, sometime, on that stage we each will play a leading role.

In the loneliness of repressed grief I found my own tendency to run. My father was my best friend. He was fifty-three years old when I was born. This muscular, quiet-spoken, town blacksmith was never sick. His presence displayed strength; his silver hair and definite facial features represented the essence of maturity to me. When he spoke I wanted to listen. Then gradually heart disease and blood clots restricted him to a hospital room and a bed. In a matter of a few weeks his strength faded, his features saddened, and early one spring morning his days of life ended. I thought I grieved. I cried. I felt alone.

Within twenty-four hours following the funeral I was back in the college classroom. Exam time was only days away. For the next nine years I ran a fast and steady pace in quest of three degrees. Life was primarily academic. Near the end of residence work on my Doctor of Theology degree an unleashed flood of new feelings inundated me. Gradually, I felt drowned in a dark night of my soul. I searched for the cause: a spiritual crisis, the impact of the times, a possible wrong choice of vocation, sin? But none of these reasons satisfied my search. I had to go way back to Dad's weeks of pain and suffering and the hopelessness I felt as I watched him die.

Yes, he had died and been buried with full military rites. Nevertheless, I had not allowed his going to be part of my life. I had never allowed him to be absent. James, Junior, had not turned James, Senior, loose. In the new loneliness of becoming free from repressed grief, I discovered my own tendency to escape. Reluctantly, I entered that category of the human race called runners, but more descriptively, escapists. And I did not like my title.

Thank God I quickly learned I was only one person in an old category, as old as Adam. The creation story in Genesis 1—2 is a beautiful and even romantic account of two people being given life's best start. Purposely, the original couple overstepped the boundary set by God. They attempted to assert themselves beyond God's prescribed limits. In rebellion against their own created natures they sought to be like their Creator. This venture in opposition was a futile and evidently frustrating try to escape their own humanness. The resistance was an attempt to be their own gods. All sin is an escape. The thief, adulterer, liar, assassin—each is primarily asserting dissatisfaction with the real and "as is" conditions of life. Thus the sinner acts in his own selfish behalf to transform reality more to his own satisfaction. The horror of Jim Jones and Guyana is a lingering and terrifying reminder of the tragedy such escapism can bring forth.

According to Scripture, subsequent generations of the Genesis couple did not profit from the lesson of the first attempted escape in Eden. Cain was unable to affirm God's acceptance of his brother Abel. Thus he could not celebrate the existence of his brother. Even the patience to tolerate Abel was absent in Cain. Desperately, Cain struck out against Abel to escape from the reminder that his brother was accepted by God. Still the end of the denial of reality had not been reached by Cain. God asked the murderer "Where is Abel your brother?" (Gen. 4:9a). The hardened escapist answered with a lie and a question for rhetorical debate. "Am I my brother's keeper?" (Gen. 4:9b). He denied reality known only to himself. Each occasion of escape is always a refusal to face a bit of private truth. My sin has an element of truth no one else can comprehend. Such a sentence, paragraph, or even chapter is for my intimate diary alone. So often, however, I play the game of denial with the truth that only I know.

And then, along came Noah. Once he was the only good man of his time. Yet, he became the first drunk recorded in the Bible. Apparently, he experimented and became enthralled with his own wine and gradually fell victim to a new and welcome feeling that removed him from a world being refurbished amidst decay and destruction. He became anesthetized and intoxicated beyond his ability to control himself. The stupor granted him the license to commit an embarrassing and shameful act.

Even Abraham resorted to escapism. The first great explorer moved day by day and step by step with God and God's covenant promise of protection and blessing. Nearing Egypt he allowed the pain of suspicion to give birth to a foolish fear for his own life. Forgetting God's promise, he plotted to pass his wife off as his sister to protect himself. The lie was a selfish ploy manufactured to ensure his own protection.

The list goes on. The list never ends. And I keep coming back to Jonah. Somewhere in the crowd of runners he stands by himself. By the way, how did we ever receive his story? Yes, God preserved the drama. But who else but the preacher of Nineveh could have given that testimony? Could it be that he is not only a biblical model of warning about escapism but also an example of the courage to confess "I ran"?

Once I realized the "running" behavior of some of these biblical folk, I was better able to face my own anxiety about escapism. I knew I was not afflicted with a new disease. People have always been running away. By accepting my own escapist traits I began to see the ships of Joppa more plainly. Each had a name.

Dreamer.—The land of dreams is forever close by. Minutes into sleep the struggle between the conscious and subconscious can initiate a drama beyond description that has the power to frighten, arouse, taunt, or please. Dreams are not to be condemned. Repeatedly, God used dreams. The Joseph story reveals the value of dreams and God's great purpose for Israel. Nevertheless, the tendency to dream while appearing to be awake is dangerous. The Land of Oz cannot be pinpointed on any map. No yellow brick road has been marked out. No blueprints exist for Shangri-La.

The good old days.—Date your own golden age. I am forty-one years old. Since 1941 my era has included World War II, Korea, Vietnam, the social discontent of the sixties, the hostage crisis in Iran, seasons of family illness, continued apathy and discontent in churches, and increasing inflation. True, these characteristics were not the total climate of any season in my life. However, to repeat any month would include muddling through some events and dilemmas I would just as soon forget. I cannot date a single period for the golden age of my past.

Tomorrowland.—Scarlett O'Hara could only partially accept the end of her relationship with Rhett Butler. Capturing the numbness in Scarlett's mind and emotions Margaret Mitchell made her say, "I won't think of it now. . . . I'll go crazy if I think about losing him now, I'll think of it tomorrow." Later Scarlett revealed her obsession, "Tomorrow, I'll think of some way to get him back. After all, tomorrow is another day."[1]

Activism.—The range extends from the frustration and drive of the workaholic to the executive with a shortened workweek trying frantically to stay busy.

Carlyle Marney believed our worship of activity had produced what he labeled contrived distractions. He told a story of a man going to see his neighbor one afternoon. A little boy answered the door and the man asked, "Where is your father?" The child answered, "He is playing golf." The neighbor proceeded to question the child as to the whereabouts of the other family members. All were involved in a variety of activities. Finally he asked the youngster, "Well, what are you doing at home?" "Mister, I wouldn't be at home except I've got the tomcat in the freezer trying to turn him into a polar bear."[2] In the absence of purposeful activity we will invent our contrived distractions.

Religion.—Watch out! You can easily be shanghaied on that ship. The two most productive money-making undertakings in America today are religion and fast foods. People are easy touches for quick foods that appease hunger and religions that give pat answers to threatening problems. The popularity of the term "born again" has outdistanced the understanding of the New Testament meaning. Ecclesiastical charlatans are legion, and mass-media productions clothed in Hollywood settings and Madison Avenue advertisements are proclaiming a limited gospel with little appreciation for the cost of discipleship.

Today, I still visit the harbor of Joppa. I must; I keep seeing ships there I have never seen before.

Encounter: The Possible Alternative

Running away always involves selling out to some degree of fantasy. A friend could verbalize all the danger signs of stress in his marriage but consistently sighed "things will work out." The divorce was nasty. A church member whispered "Time heals all things" as she embraced the mother in front of three caskets holding the bodies of her three high school sons, victims of a drunk driver. Life includes harsh realities, and attempts to ignore or abandon trouble, allowing it to be simply part of the passing of time, are futile.

I gently probed to try to find the reason for the young executive's obsession to succeed. He stopped me cold. "Maybe someday I'll let someone in." He opted to delay one of life's most worthy discoveries—himself. Rip Van Winkle slept quietly and undisturbed for twenty years. His season of slumber paralleled the birth of the American Revolution, and he missed that adventure.

The "super person" traveling with the attitude that he has conquered all reality has shored himself up with blocks of sand. His imposed judgment is a disguise as fragile as a china cup. He has never met all reality, and to announce how he would respond in any given dilemma is, in fact, taking himself for granted.

All of these are the same. They are various shades of fantasy that are seemingly pregnant with the potential to limit, rob, and destroy God-given life and its fullest possibilities.

Actually, eternally, we cannot escape life. Jesus told a story featuring three men who received varying numbers of talents. Each of the three was graced with equal accountability for his gifts. Two used their presents responsibly and with gratitude. The third fell victim to his emotions, sulked in self-pity and fear, dug a hole, and buried his talent. Responsibilities are not discharged just because we put them out of sight. Jesus affirmed this nonnegotiable truth quite clearly: "For nothing is hidden, except to be revealed; nor has anything been secret, but that it should come to light" (Mark 4:22).

Ultimately we each face judgment. According to Jesus each person's entire life will be reviewed in the great judgment. Assuredly, within the scope of such an inevitable audit and review, we will be confronted with our seasons of escape.

We are wise to remember Jonah. He did run away. He fallaciously reasoned that distance could remove him from God. But even locked in his remorse and the guilt of believing his rebellious act had brought on a storm, he could not even die to escape. No final or eternal escapism existed for the prophet. In the very belly of the deep, an experience depicting the ultimate depth of his escape, he could no longer flee from reality. Jonah in distress, a vulnerable victim of deep and treacherous water, fearful of losing consciousness, and cognizant of possible impending agony worse than death, prayed. In his inescapable moment, fixed in place, having no space for further escape, he faced God. When we exhaust our running room, the ultimate reality of God abides.

Jonah was graced by the patient and loving Lord with another opportunity. Therein is our hope. Jonah's encounter is a living testimony to the possibility for conversion, passing from escapism to encounter.

From Escape to Encounter: A Perennial Vigil

How do we face up instead of running away?

Choose to face life.—Jonah's realization begins: "Then Jonah prayed to the Lord his God from the stomach of the fish" (Jonah 2:1). The remainder of the chapter is a poetic and prayerful description of his understanding of his dilemma. In his inescapable moment Jonah made a new choice. We do not have to wait for the hour of desperation to begin to face life. All the warning of the prophet's message is a cry to us to face life before tragedy faces us.

Remember, you are not alone!—Probably the greatest struggle in facing reality is the fear of facing up alone. Through faith in God we choose to believe we are not alone. By faithing God, we come to know his realness, aliveness, personalness, and his caring and understanding of our needs. We also relax in knowing that we were not created to handle life alone. Besides, God created us. He knows all reality. He never runs from his creation. Only God never sets sail from Joppa.

Jesus had the opportunity to run. According to Luke, as the cross drew near, Jesus "stedfastly set his face to go to Jerusalem" (Luke 9:51, KJV). He could have turned down another road. He could have waited outside Jerusalem. He could have run away. Instead, firmly he set his face toward his destiny—fulfilling the will of the Father on the cross. His responsible act enables me to know that I am not alone in facing my life.

Manifest your courage.—"Caesar" was there in those months of my personal struggle. Caesar was my tomcat. He liked to travel at night. Many mornings he would come home bleeding, scratched, and cut—scars and wounds received during his nightly excursions. Just as often as he was wounded, so often I hurried him to the vet. His escapades became a topic of humorous conversation. One morning while treating Caesar the vet asked, "Have you noticed anything peculiar about his wounds?" He quickly answered his own question. "He always gets hurt on the head. This cat has never been injured running away from a fight." My Caesar's actions preached a sermon on courage. I mused on that experience as I felt the spring of courage begin to flow into my life.

Be patient.—The change from running from life to meeting life may not come quickly. Old patterns of escapism will continue to linger, haunt, and tempt. A perfect record of encountering may not follow the decision to face life. We probably will run again. Even following his crusade in Nineveh, Jonah ran again. He sulked in displeasure over the city's repentance. He harbored a feeling of vindictiveness and went outside the city unable to celebrate God's grace upon Nineveh. But as the book closes, God is speaking to Jonah. God had not abandoned the runner.

Believe in a greater purpose.—Several years ago the executive secretary of the Mississippi Baptist Convention, Dr. Chester Quarles, died suddenly while on a missionary tour of South America. Several days later, at the funeral, Dr. Douglas Hudgins, then pastor of the First Baptist Church of Jackson, Mississippi, began his memorial tribute with these words:

> Everyone of us in this room would like to go over to some corner and sit down and cry over the loss of our friend, 'Ches' Quarles. But 'Ches' would not have us do this. He would beckon us to move on and out into further ventures in the service of Jesus Christ.

To run away is always the easier of the two options. To sail away on a select ship from Joppa is sometimes attractive. The ships will always be waiting to sail.

Notes

1. Margaret Mitchell, *Gone with the Wind* (New York: The Macmillan Co., 1936), p. 719.

2. Carlyle Marney, *Beggars in Velvet* (New York: Abingdon Press, 1960), p. 18.

2
My Season for Struggle Never Closes

Let's pretend!

You have the opportunity to redesign life. What would you eliminate? Death, hunger, taxes, fear, mosquitoes, potholes? Each is a threat. Would you also include struggles in your renovation of life?

Struggle:

the battle for meaning when worthy purposes seem swallowed up in emptiness;

the strain for courage against fears and threats;

the effort to salvage peace and joy when bombarded by the agony of conflict and distress;

the fight to make sense of pain that seems immune to medicine;

the tension to keep faith when God seems silent;

the conflict of feelings that mix joy and sorrow, hope and despair, love and hate, fear and courage;

the contest of will against the weight of apathy;

the pull to be versus the power to act.

But before you become caught up in the fantasy of license to erase all human striving, remember there is another side to struggle.

The April morning in Middle Tennessee came clear, bright, and warm. Quickly a blanket of clouds shrouded the sky. Snow began to fall. Once the ground was covered in white, the clouds quickly vanished and the golden sun melted the snow. The snow had hardly disappeared before the clouds rolled in again and white flakes swirled down in blizzard fashion. Again the ground was paved in white. The sun emerged from the clouds, and the snow melted away. Throughout that entire April day this intriguing and mystifying process was repeated until finally as night fell, the sun set in the clear sky. Winter had struggled to stay alive. Spring had fought to be born. Neither, for that day, could surrender. Such wrestling of the seasons is only part of God's creative order.

While laboring patiently to improve the electric battery, Thomas Edison observed that an electric current passing through a strip of carbon paper turned the strip almost white and gave off light. Convinced that this procedure could produce light, he tackled a series of obstacles blocking his way to develop the electric light. A method to deliver electricity to potential customers and the invention of the glass bulb to house the light were completed, but the frustrating quest to discover a long burning and inexpensive filament lingered. He tried platinum, boron, osmium, and varieties of bamboo and vegetable fibers. Finally, after fourteen months of tests and experiments in a secluded laboratory he produced a carbon filament, both durable and inexpensive.[1] The genius of man is always a product of his persistent labor.

Our Lord struggled alone in prayer in Gethsemane. According to Matthew, Jesus "began to be grieved and distressed" (Matt. 26:37b). He called out, "My Father, if it is possible, let this cup pass from me." The intensity of the struggle was revealed as he continued "yet not as I will, but as Thou wilt" (Matt. 26:39). The desires, wants, and wishes of the Father and the Son met in Scripture's highest peak of prayer. For Jesus this was no resignation, no fantasy, no denial, but reality born out of struggle.

Yes, changing seasons require the conflict of the elements.

Yes, man benefits from the perseverance of the inventor.

Yes, we bow in reverence to the encounter completed in Gethsemane by our Christ.

But my struggle is day by day, every day. Sometime, every day, I hurt from toil. I strain to spread my time to all my family. I endeavor to harmonize feeling, thought, and will. These contentions and others do not come and go; they are continually in attendance.

However, I need not despair. There is another, one of apostolic credentials, who gives testimony to the same reality. He ministers to my ongoing struggle.

Paul Kept in Touch with His Struggle

The origin of Paul's struggle is a mystery. Did Gamaliel's masterful teachings challenge him to think and initiate some dissatisfaction with his rabbinical upbringing? Had Paul begun to feel threatened by the bonds of love and unity exemplified in the young Christian community? Could the testimony of the dying Stephen committing himself into the care of the Lord Jesus have touched the soul of Saul? The degree of struggle is in question. But we realize that the vicious persecutor, leaving Jerusalem intent on destroying the disciples of the Lord, was absorbed in conflict.

Nearing Damascus the rising crescendo of the struggle peaked as God moved in at the opportune moment. The bold Hebrew, jealous to eradicate any challenge to Jewish tradition, was knocked down and stopped cold. God spoke pointedly to Paul's vulnerable and exposed spot—rage vented in the obsession to persecute Christians. His desperation to know who was speaking was answered as the living Christ declared his presence. Moments before Saul had been the self-sufficient champion of the law of his fathers. Now he was blinded and was led by the hand into the Syrian city to exist in a mesmerized state, unable to eat and drink. Visibly, he was docile, quiet, and unprepossessing. Inwardly, the mature orthodox Jew on a journey to eradicate a religious sect, the menace to his religious system, and the Lord Jesus Christ were sparring for direction and dominance. During this season of struggle God sent in the timid and fearful, but willing, Ananias. This disciple's word spoken in the authority of the living Christ brought sight and peace to Paul.

Years later as he wrote to the Christians of the Galatian region, Paul included an autobiographical note, quite germane to our understanding of his struggle. Outlining his early spiritual life he wrote, "Nor did I go up to Jerusalem to those who were apostles before me; but I went away to Arabia" (Gal. 1:17). Why such a trip? Why then? Paul's Arabian visit, however long, is generally and traditionally considered as a time for retreat, an interval of meditation and reflection. But remember the man? His life had been absorbed in the bonds of a religion that had shut out the non-Jews of the world. This same set of beliefs was meticulously bound in tradition and maintained control of the people by imposing trivial restrictions. Paul who had lived under the sway of such religious dictates had encountered the liberating, alive, and revealed Christ. But Paul was a scholar and serious student, and that side of his personality could not be denied. The radical personal change he experienced demanded a getaway time to think and pray. Arabia was for Paul as the back side of the desert was for Moses and as Saturdays in prayer at Wittenberg were for Luther. As the seed of the good news of Christ was germinating, the apostle-to-be had to get away to study his soil.

Paul was revealing a choice in Galatians. The more natural expectation would have been to return to Jerusalem and the small Christian community there. But Paul's venture into Arabia was a willful decision to be alone in a sparsely populated territory. He chose to enter into this struggle. Maturity is evident in such a choice. On the road to Damascus struggle met him, but by going to Arabia he chose his own struggle.

Following the Arabian encounter the struggles continued. In fact, tension seemed to travel with Paul.

Evidence of his accompanying struggles—the gospel warring with sin, opposing tradition, and prevailing pagan influences—was demonstrated vividly in the missionary's visit to Philippi.

Macedonia was God's priority for Paul, winning out over the apostle's earlier choice to go to Bithynia. In Philippi the testimony of the way of salvation proved a threat to profit-minded masters of a slave girl. Paul's compassionate ministry to her resulted in both him and Silas being beaten, jailed, and placed in stocks. Their convictions sustained them, even enabling the duo to sing praises unto God while incarcerated in a hideous dungeon. A sudden earthquake heightened their anxiety but provided an opportunity to bear testimony to the jailer. As a result, the jailer's entire family received Christ. Yet even as city magistrates expressed a change of heart, the general tension caused by the apostle's presence overrode the hospitality of the city. Cognizant of the conditions, the missionaries left town. The Philippian adventure remains a single illustration of Paul's ongoing struggle.

We applaud Paul for making a date with himself in Arabia.

We are refreshed by his consistency and determination in the sequence of events in Philippi.

We are thankful that tucked into the interior of Romans, that gospel according to Paul, is the apostle's boldness to lay bare the very depth of his struggle. Romans 7 is usually read too quickly. Too easily we give in to the temptation to debate the chapter—is Paul referring to the redeemed or unredeemed? Can we not allow the great apostle, missionary to the Gentiles, apostolic theologian, scholarly churchman, to have his human moment amidst heavy doctrine?

Listen to him.

> For that which I am doing, I do not understand; for I am not practicing what I would like to do, but I am doing the very thing I hate. For I know that nothing good dwells in me, that is, in my flesh; for the wishing is present in me, but the doing of the good is not. For the good that I wish, I do not do; but I practice the very evil that I do not wish. But if I am doing the very thing I do not wish, I am no longer the one doing it, but sin which dwells in me. I find then the principle that evil is present in me, the one who wishes to do good. For I joyfully concur with the law of God in the inner man." (Rom. 7:15,18-21)

Why this now?

This confession was written by a man radically different from the broken convert on the road to Damascus, the new disciple sorting out his beliefs in Arabia, or even the victim of the fears of city fathers of Philippi.

Paul was confessing to his own personal stress in being pulled in opposite directions. He acknowledged the inner frustration of a perennial civil war as a man able to see what is good, yet unable always to do the good; able to recognize wrong, but unable always to refrain from wrongdoing. The evangelist, writing from Corinth his classic of the Christian faith that testifies to righteousness by faith, included his personal witness that simultaneously we can be haunted by sin and attracted to goodness.

Such an admittance does not seem easy. Quite the contrary, this intimate disclosure was an act of inner strength and courage for Paul. Only because the struggle had brought growth and maturity and because of the presence of the Holy Spirit could Paul include this bold exposure.

Paul Did Not Struggle Alone

Once Paul bared the naked truth of his struggle (Rom. 7) he set a question before himself, the Roman Christians, and each of us. "Who will set me free from the body of this death?" (Rom. 7:24).

A "wretched man" was crying out. The label depicting his condition signaled the presence of prolonged misery, hardship, and distress. His state of being did not include the remorse of guilt. Paul was describing emotional strife connected with the presence of struggle. He was not reporting the result of his sin.

The question is always there, never rhetorical or even debatable, but forever personal. Such a question is the incessant cue that the dynamic struggle never ceases.

The question cannot be ignored. The presence of the question necessitates, at least, an attempt to search for an answer.

Can enough knowledge enable me to handle my struggle?

I attempt to play golf. I know to keep my head down, but the temptation and habit often win out. God's Word is plain. Gossip, envy, and jealousy are sins. But we indulge.

Can sufficient willpower give me victory over my struggles?

Peter was determined. "Even if I have to die with You, I will not deny You!" (Mark 14:31). But by the time the rooster announced the dawn Peter had denied the Lord Jesus three times.

Can adequate emotional stability prevent my struggle from wrecking me?

Emotions fluctuate. Feelings rise and fall as the tides. Life always includes unforeseen events with accompanying new stresses. Besides, when is sufficient emotional stability reached?

Can ample strength defeat all my struggles? Remember Samson?

Such props are inadequate for the weight of the load. Besides, Paul offered a radically different answer.

"Thanks be to God through Jesus Christ our Lord!" (Rom. 7:25). Gratitude is expressed for something received. The struggling man, Paul, had welcomed the presence of God into his life. He had made room for the living Christ in his struggle. Jesus was Lord in his struggle. Even as he was acutely aware of his ongoing misery he quickly announced his understanding that he was not left to struggle alone. Gratitude, heartfelt appreciation, thankful praise, all were included in Paul's answer to his own question. The living Lord had sustained him and would bear him up in his continued struggle.

Despair, remorse, bitterness, and defeat are all absent in Paul's response to struggle. Once the darkened loneliness of struggle fades, value and meaning in the tension of life begin to dawn. This is possible because of God's presence in the struggle and the undeniable fact that he abides in the midst of worthwhile happenings. Our struggle matters to God.

On the anticipated eve of the Battle of Britain Prime Minister Winston Churchill addressed the nation by radio, "Let us . . .

brace ourselves to our duties, and so bear ourselves that, if the British empire and its Commonwealth last for a thousand years, men will still say, 'This was their finest hour.' "[2]

Churchill was not labeling the victory, he was anticipating the struggle. My season for struggle just may be my finest hour.

Notes

1. Matthew Josephson, *Edison* (New York: McGraw-Hill Book Co., Inc., 1963), pp. 205-222.

2. Abraham Rothbert, "Siege" in *Eyewitness History of World War II* (New York: Bantam Books, Inc.), 2:12.

3
I Can't Blame My Sin on Any Snake

"The devil made me do it."

Humorist Flip Wilson's comic cop-out is today's tragedy.

The temptation to place blame is alluring. In no area of life is this more evident than the human drift toward irresponsibility for sin.

Sin—the word encompasses an extraordinary range of ideas, some quite unhealthy. A child fears that his disobedience will place a black mark by his name in "God's big book." A lady feels "out of the Spirit" for her transgressions of wearing a bikini, reading lurid novels, and drinking the cooking sherry. And finally, the judgmental definition—sin is what you do that I do not do and that I disagree with. All of these statements are meant with some intended degree of integrity as attempts to define or identify sin.

Society left unchecked can continually drift toward apathy concerning error and iniquity. Carl Menninger discovered in his study of "American sin" that from 1953 to 1972 no American President used the word *sin* in a public address. Menninger noted, "So, as a nation, we officially ceased 'sinning' some twenty years ago."[1] During that era I asked a large group of youth at Glorieta Baptist Conference Center to list their primary spiritual problem and/or perplexing question concerning the Christian faith. Not one person mentioned the word *sin*. Even though this analysis describes conditions of a society over a decade ago, our feet can slide again so easily into another "sinless" life-style.

Sin—the human debris left by the damaging effects of malicious and heinous selfish acts continues to grow. A wife is brutally beaten. A precious child is sexually molested. A senior adult couple is swindled out of their life's savings. A family is abandoned by a father and husband. A soldier of a war long past carries the unresolved guilt of killing a civilian. A released convict lives with the psychological wounds inflicted during prison. Enough! Each day's newspaper is another commentary on the effects of sin.

While the quest for a definition of sin, caution concerning apathy toward sin, and cognizance of the consequences of sin, all must be repeatedly sounded, I must give priority consideration to my bent toward escaping the blame for my sin.

When I refuse blame for my sin I resign myself to the status of victim and cry, "Exploited! Framed! Used!"

When I deny blame for my sin I often substitute excuse for the sin to salve my conscience.

When I reject blame for my sin I lie to myself and aim another shattering blow at my personal integrity.

When I decline blame for my sin I attempt to exclude myself from accountability for the consequences of my sin.

When I refuse to accept blame for my sin I endeavor in fantasy to absolve myself of my own guilt.

Because such attempts eat away the human quality of responsibility like an aggressive malignancy, immediate treatment is demanded to initiate the onset of remission and possible recovery.

Life Is Both Wheat Field and Weed Patch

Personal good and evil will remain with us as long as the world exists. Such a nonnegotiable fact cannot be denied. Each biblical author wrote from the conviction that sin exists, and Jesus declared the undeniable reality that *people* participate in the ongoing conflict of good and evil (Matt. 13:24-30).

A farmer carefully prepared his field and planted fresh, bright, and dry seed. With planting completed, he went home to wait out the growing process. A few nights later someone carrying a sack of seed visited the planted field. The visitor's seed, while similar in size to those already planted, were dull, gray, and smelled musty. Darnel! This weed, breaking through the sod, resembled wheat. But not only was it a "pretender," it was also potentially poisonous. Only later as the plant began to head was its true identity known. Some mysterious person had sown weeds in a good field.

One day a group of servants, possibly those who originally planted the field, noticed the unusual and unexpected growth. Alarmed, they hurried to tell their master. He quickly summed up the situation, "An enemy has done this" (v. 28). The kingdom parable showed the harsh truth that the world is both wheat field and weed patch. Jesus was not delivering a lecture on agriculture. He was describing the inevitable vying of good and evil in human beings.

Why does this tension exist? Often we ask the question as an easy and cheap academic ploy to satisfy the need to place blame. Besides, time used analyzing the origin and cause of evil is time spent not tending to the consequences of our own sins. Jesus never addressed the origin or reason for conflict. His immediate concern was to press home the point that human beings intentionally both commit evil and do good. No person is immune. Each of us plants both good seeds and weed seed along the pilgrimage of life. Such is our undeniable mixture.

Consider two Old Testament pioneers of faith. Joseph certainly could have planted the tares of bitterness and hostility toward his brothers who had sold him into slavery. Instead, he literally gave them wheat from his own seed in a time of famine.

Esther could have reaped from the seed of apathy and noninvolvement. Instead the queen agonized and bore fruit from the seed of love for her people. The temptation to plant either seed abides. Again, this is an undeniable human reality. To claim exemption is to deny one's humanity. And that in itself is a severe sin.

Now return to the wisdom of the Master. The surprised and

concerned servants were advised to wait for the harvest. The weeds would be allowed to grow with the wheat. But the weeds would not triumph. Quite the contrary, the harvested darnel would be gathered to be destroyed! The harvested wheat would be relieved of the nuisance of the weeds. Daily life involves the presence of temptation and even participation in evil. But such discord is ultimately only seasonal; God is not going to permit evil to be a permanent force in his universe.

The need to blame, which is a refusal to be accountable for personal evil acts, arises partially out of the fear of the power and influence of our personal sins. But such power and influence cannot be victorious in the life of the redeemed of God.

The Irresponsible Tendency: Who's to Blame?

Only if you are ready to accept the earthly personal tension of good and evil are you prepared to consider a hard and realistic look at your own bent toward blaming your sin on someone or something else.

Biblical teaching concerning sin, private experiences of temptation to do wrong, personal consequences of our own sin, and knowledge of atrocities caused by sin, all lead us to readily conclude that something other than good exists. Even so, the undeniable tendency to waive responsibility, relinquish liability, and disclaim accountability for sin and attest to being ruled by forces or influence beyond personal control prevails. Such a tendency has always existed.

Two trees in Eden primarily held the attention of Adam and Eve (Gen. 2:9). The tree of life represented God's ample and gracious provision for human life. The tree of the knowledge of good and evil represented the restrictions and limitations which God imposed on human life. Man was not ready for certain wisdom, insights, and knowledge, and so God drew a boundary.

Soon the tempter began his maneuvering and deceitfully aroused Eve's suspicion concerning the restrictions. A restriction always offers an enticing challenge. Curiosity, doubt, and intrigue won out. The couple stepped beyond God's limits. In rebelling against God's boundaries they sinned.

Presently God offered an opportunity for the couple to confess to overstepping his prescribed limits and breaking into denied territory.

Their response was the first venture in blame.

Adam censured Eve. Eve charged the guilt to the snake.

The snake did plant the seeds of doubt, suspicion, and enticement, but once God dealt with the serpent he proceeded to call man to accountability.

In the moments when God's attention and wrath were turned on the snake, possibly Adam breathed easier in a short season of reprieve. But it was quite short. God came back to instruct Adam in a fact of life. Yes, he could be influenced by the tempter, but this was no license. "Adam, what you sow you also reap." Genesis 1—3 reveals the wonders and magnificence of creation, the great potential of man, and the entrance of sin. If we stop there we are unprepared to go on into life. We must see God's displeasure and intolerance of our tendency to place the blame elsewhere.

Today we still snake hunt. Consider some of the snakes we blame:

Environment—Even though Lot's wife never cut her ties with the culture of Sodom, her act of turning back was her own choice (see Gen. 19:26). Paul certainly grieved over the inability of Demas to follow the call of missions, but in his letter to Timothy, he emphatically labeled Demas' desertion as a chosen action (2 Tim. 4:10). Neither the ambivalent wife or the unfaithful missionary could plead innocence.

Bad blood—"Ahaziah the son of Ahab became king over Israel. . . . And he did evil in the sight of the Lord and walked in the way of his father and in the way of his mother and in the way of Jeroboam the son of Nebat who caused Israel to sin. So he served Baal and worshiped him and provoked the Lord God of

Israel to anger according to all that his father had done" (1 Kings 22:51-53). Who could present a better case for an inherited evil? The Scriptures never dismiss his accountability.

Rationalism—Jonah resorted to logic in his prayer to vindicate himself and express his displeasure over Nineveh's repentance (Jonah 4:1 ff.). And God challenged the validity of his reasoning.

Circumstances—The prodigal son's elder brother attempted to convince his father and himself that his need to stay home, serve the family, and keep the father's commands gave him the right not to accept his brother (Luke 15:29). Luke does not record any account of the resolution of this sin.

Fate—The man with the single talent attempted to assign to himself the title "Shortchanged" (Matt. 25:24). He lost all.

And the snake hunt goes on.

Our Responsible Option: I Have Sinned

But this pass-the-buck generation is not locked in. The Old Testament account of the resolution of David's sin is a live testimony that we have another option.

King David committed adultery. To cover Bathsheba's resulting pregnancy he devised a plot that backfired and ultimately resulted in the murder of Uriah. The series of events actually began when David should have been at the front line of battle (2 Sam. 11:1). During David's idleness, Bathsheba's beauty captured the king, and he used her for his selfish sexual desires. David, as Adam and Eve and all others, violated God's boundaries and limits.

Possibly I am being too harsh. Maybe David was a victim of circumstances. If there had been no war and Uriah had been at home, David possibly would have escaped temptation.

My father never understood my rationale for taking Mrs. Winstead's pears. Any pear tree with limbs loaded with ripe fruit hanging over a sidewalk in reach of a bicycle rider is a circumstance beyond the control of a twelve-year-old American boy. But Dad just couldn't see the incident from that perspective.

Well, David thought the matter was sealed away. Uriah had died in battle, and David married Bathsheba.

But along came Nathan. God sent him into the drama. God and Nathan captured the adulterous and murderous king's attention with a tragic story. A rich man with flocks and herds took a pet lamb from a poor man to feed a guest. David burned with indignation and rage for the unjust atrocity. His anger subsided when Nathan, apparently calm and direct, said, "You are the man" (2 Sam. 12:7). Nathan expounded on his text by reminding David of God's blessing to him, recounted the heinous sin, and forecast coming judgment on the king. And David, the shepherd lad who received God's comforting presence on the hillsides of Judea, the boy warrior who fought Goliath with God's power, as a mighty monarch experienced the moral justice of the same God.

"I have sinned against the Lord" (2 Sam. 12:13). A wise man knows when to confess his sins. The writer of 2 Samuel narrates the subsequent events: the sickness and death of David's son; the king's remorse; and, ultimately, the renewal of hope. However, the essence of the pathos and agony of the confession is not contained in the narration. Later David, more in control of his emotions, but indelibly mindful of the trauma, wrote down his suffering.

> Be gracious to me, O God, according to Thy loving-kindness;
> According to the greatness of Thy compassion blot out my transgressions.
> Wash me thoroughly from my iniquity,
> And cleanse me from my sin.
> For I know my transgressions,
> And my sin is ever before me.
> . . . .
> Make me hear joy and gladness,
> Let the bones which Thou hast broken rejoice.
> Hide Thy face from my sins,
> And blot out all my iniquities.
> Create in me a clean heart, O God,
> And renew a steadfast spirit within me.
> Do not cast me away from Thy presence,
> And do not take Thy Holy Spirit from me.

Restore to me the joy of Thy salvation,
And sustain me with a willing spirit (Ps. 51:1-3, 8-12).

Confession of sin is not words alone. Sin is an act of the total person. Responsible admission of guilt involves more than rote words and must reach to the very marrow of the soul. Sin destroys health because the accompanying guilt visits life with a unique stress that eats away at the moral, emotional, mental, psychological, and spiritual parts of life.

When I blame my sin on you or any event or any circumstance I attempt to deny the disease that will kill me. "For the wages of sin is death" (Rom. 6:23). And we are ultimately faced with the only alternative: "Who can forgive sins, but God alone?" (Luke 5:21).

Note

1. Karl Menninger, *Whatever Became of Sin* (New York: Hawthorn Books, Inc., 1973), p. 15.

4

There Is No Bridge Over My Troubled Waters

As the seventies began songwriters Paul Simon and Art Garfunkel wrote and released a haunting ballad entitled "Bridge Over Troubled Water." The song gave hope following the previous decade of protest and unrest. The refrain of the song suggested help for the existing maladies—the supposedly existent "bridge over troubled waters." Today that musical composition is an abiding classic. It did not describe an era that passed away; rather the lyrics narrated two perennial and personal concerns. First, affliction does visit each person. Second, each person desires relief or deliverance from the grievous burdens of life. In addition, a closer analysis of the stanzas reveals that the text is a combination of both fact and fantasy concerning our human response to affliction.

First, the ballad is a song about *the fact or condition of human affliction*. Probably all of us know what it is to awaken to the dawn of a blue Monday—or Tuesday or Wednesday. No one is exempt from the pressures that accompany life changes through the aging process. Sometimes added responsibilities on the daily job or in the home seem quite unfair, especially when you believe you have all the liability you can handle. Usually the anguish of living in the aftermath of a bad decision brings some disruption to life. Rejection can surface when promotion time arrives and you are overlooked.

Church people share together many afflictions. These include lengthy illnesses that often intensify in pain and expense. Occasionally, family communication in the church is shut off, and you are saddled with a strange spiritual loneliness. There are seasons when the grief situations that we share together as the body of Christ become increasingly heavy even with our attempts to nurture and care for one another.

In our modern society marital crises increasingly threaten the bonds of families. Job change can require emotional as well as intellectual transition.

All of these varying degrees of trauma attest to the fact that affliction is part of the human drama of life. In turn, we each face our moment or season of questioning. Can we see it through? Inevitably, we compare ourselves with others who have similar burdens. We conclude that certain people are never burdened with life, and thus we cry out, "Oh God, why me? Why can I not be released from this trial?" The fact, the cold reality, is that affliction visits all of us at some time of life. Trouble is part of living.

On the other hand, the Simon and Garfunkel hit is a *fantasy concerning affliction. There is no bridge over troubled water.* If we are true to our Christian calling and to the message of Scripture we must recognize that God by his presence makes possible paths *through*; he does not build bridges *over*. To bridge over would be to attempt to move beyond or around existing trouble. The Bible is clear from the conflict of Cain and Abel through the struggles of Paul that God makes paths through; he does not build bridges over. Consider two Old Testament illustrations of this truth.

Picture the children of Israel encamped by the Red Sea. Grasp their dilemma. The same pharaoh who earlier was beaten into submission and awarded them freedom had a change of heart. He questioned his act of emancipation and initiated a pursuit of the released nation. He gathered all his chariots and, dominated by a hardened heart, boldly chased after the Israelites.

The Hebrews, still basking in the light of new freedom, were startled to see the advancing Egyptian army. In fear, they cried to God. In anger, they blamed Moses. The army was hastily approaching. The barrier of water was in front, and to run to either

side would have been to expend energy in a futile effort. But
Moses stood firm. "Do not fear! Stand by and see the salvation of
the Lord which He will accomplish for you today; for the Egyp-
tians whom you have seen today, you will never see them again
forever" (Ex. 14:13).

God, out of his desire to deliver the people and in response to
Moses' faith, instructed the emancipator to command the people
to go forward.

To Moses he commanded, "Lift up your staff and stretch out
your hand over the sea and divide it, and the sons of Israel shall
go through the midst of the sea on dry land" (Ex. 14:16). Moses
obeyed the Lord. All through the night God used a strong east
wind to divide the sea, and the next morning a path of dry land
lay exposed.

On either side stood a mountainous wall of water. "And the
sons of Israel went through the midst of the sea on the dry land"
(Ex. 14:22).

God could have acted differently.

God who makes dry paths through the sea could have heaved
up a dirt bridge across the water.

God who makes dry paths through the sea could have destroyed
the pursuing army and given Israel ample time to bypass the
water obstacle.

God who makes a dry path through the sea could have . . .

But God chose only to make a path through. Even then he
could have backed the wall of water, a challenge to the faith of the
people, away from the sight of the travelers. But he only made a
path through. A path was all that God provided. A path was
sufficient for Israel.

Daniel lived in the friendly graces of King Darius. Such
recognition created jealousy among Daniel's regal associates.
They searched to discover and expose some weakness or corrup-
tion in the interpreter of dreams. In desperation they appealed to
the vanity of Darius and persuaded him to pass a rigid law that
anyone praying to any god or man beside Darius for the next

thirty days would be thrown into the lion's den. Daniel was aware of the signed decree, but he continued his daily prayers to God. Daniel was discovered praying. The king attempted to rescind the law in Daniel's behalf, but Darius finally gave in to the pressure of his commissioners and satraps.

King Darius himself, in an emotional encounter, informed Daniel of his fate. He quickly assured the young man, "Your God whom you constantly serve will Himself deliver you" (Daniel 6:16). The king carried through his own sentence, even to sealing the stone over the lions' den in order to dispel any charge of favoritism for Daniel. The incident could have been so different.

God could have preserved Daniel from being discovered at prayer.

God could have strengthened Darius and enabled him to pardon Daniel.

God could have aided Daniel to escape from King Darius. Instead God allowed Daniel to spend the night among the lions and be released unharmed the following morning. In the midst of ferocious and carnivorous beasts, God kept his man safe through the night. He made a way through.

Naturally, as one recognizes and accepts this principle of life there is a resounding, intimate question: how will God lead me through? How can I move from the cloudy now to the dawn of sunshine and joy? The way is discovered in the life of Jesus Christ. He never tried to build a bridge over. Jesus was led by the Father through his afflictions. The life experiences of Jesus Christ are the greatest testimony to the fact that God leads us through rather than building a bridge over. On several pivotal occasions of affliction and grievous burden Christ was moved constantly through as the Father prepared a way, a path for him.

Jesus Was Led Through by Facing His Conflicts

In the agony of the temptation experience Jesus came to grips with the scope of the ministry that he was to pursue (Matt. 4:1-11).

However, in that same event he encountered the reality of facing conflict. Our Lord, being a free man, had options. He could have attempted to ignore the temptations, or he could have endeavored to fantasize about Satan. Yet he recognized this anxiety period as a time he had to accept. The same is true with us. When affliction visits us either as grief, emotional strain, or personal loss, our first calling is to face the malady and accept the fact that this is happening to us personally.

Years ago, *Harvey,* a comedy, opened on Broadway. The protagonist of the play, a character named Elwood P. Dowd, persists in communicating with a giant rabbit. In one scene Dowd talks with a psychiatrist who declares, "Mr. Dowd, you have to face reality." Elwood quickly replies, "Doctor, I wrestled with reality for forty years, and I am happy to state that I finally won out over it."[1] Such a victory is inevitably a loss.

Whether you feel a pin pricking you or live constantly with a heavy burden, accepting the reality of the pain is mandatory if you are to allow God to lead you through his path. We begin at point zero by accepting what is upon us and then ask God to move us on from that point.

Jesus Was Led Through by Being Himself

Jesus went home one day. During his visit to Nazareth he attended church, the synagogue (Luke 4:16-31). The hometown folk asked him to preach. He proclaimed the message that the time had arrived for the expected Messiah. Next he pointed out to them that on an occasion of great drought God in his miraculous manner led one of his men to a widow of Zarephath (1 Kings 17—18). He continued by reminding his hometown audience of the healing of the Syrian, Naaman, a leprous man (2 Kings 5). All of a sudden the church people reacted violently. Jesus speaking to a Jewish audience had been saying that God cares for someone besides the Jews. They could not accept that assertion. Immediately, crisis was imminent for him. Yet Jesus did not disguise himself or back down. He was transparently himself. He did not try to be something other than what he was. He was just himself in the home setting where he was reared.

You have to be yourself. There are no real supermen or superwomen. Each of us is very human. At some time we all would like to cry out, "Why does this happen to me? I am a Christian. I am above this dilemma." Come back to reality. Yes, you are on the center stage of your tragedy. You have to play your lead role.

One of the greatest artists of the Renaissance era was Buonarroti Michelangelo. When you view his work, you never realize that Michelangelo's parents beat him almost daily in an attempt to persuade him to give up art. But art was in him; art was native to him. He had to be true to himself even in the midst of cruel circumstances. John Bunyan, one of Christendom's greatest preachers, was locked away in the Bedford jail, but Bunyan was true to himself. Even though the world was locked away from him, he looked inside himself and found the plot for *The Pilgrim's Progress,* still a devotional classic. Paul tried to get away from his true self on at least three occasions when the afflictions of his life became heavy upon him. He cried out, hoping that his affliction, a thorn in the flesh, would be removed. Yet the response was always the same, "My grace is sufficient for you" (2 Cor. 12:9). Paul did not fantasize about his trouble; it was real. We have to accept our afflictions, bear up bravely, and allow our personal talents and faith in God to sustain us.

Jesus Was Led Through by Concentration on a Greater Ministry

One sabbath Jesus healed a man, but he did it on the wrong day, according to the Jews (Mark 3). He broke the "blue laws." Immediately they initiated a plot to kill him. He was aware of their scheme. Nevertheless, Jesus chose a course of action that is admirable for us. He concentrated his attention on something greater than his own problem. Jesus left the scene of potential conflict, went away, and soon began the work of selecting his disciples and training them. He concentrated his attention on preparing his followers to be effective witnesses after his earthly ministry was completed. This is our calling also. However, we must be careful that we are not pursuing a selfish higher course. It is a rule of life that focusing attention on a noble purpose, such as helping someone who is in great need, brings renewed strength. Christ found strength throughout his ministry by pouring out his life to bring health and care and meaning to other persons. In the midst of the burden we must give attention to putting our minds on something greater than ourselves.

Jesus Was Led Through by Going Away to Be Alone

One day Jesus learned that his close friend, John the Baptist, had been senselessly killed amid a carnival atmosphere. Jesus chose in the midst of his deep grief to draw aside and to be alone (Matt. 14:12-13). These moments were one of the few treasured occasions when he could just be by himself. The four Gospels reveal quite candidly the rhythm of his life. He would go into the midst of the people, serve, and then he would draw apart. He would return to the presence of the people and once again draw apart to be alone. The rhythm of life was not just a sequence reserved for him. It can be quite therapeutic for each of us. No human being who faces life realistically can face it constantly in the midst of people. Somehow, we have to find that season alone to allow the soul to be restored.

Jesus Was Led Through by the Hope of Resurrection

Jesus walked into the interior of shadowy and dark Gethsemane alone (Luke 22:41). Nearby, the disciples fell asleep. He could have gone through the garden and kept on going. Instead, he chose to stay there, and by doing so he initiated the victory that the world revolves around today, the triumph of the atonement. By choosing to stay through the affliction of his cross, through the agony of dying, and on through the tomb, he came to experience resurrection. That is the greatest meaning of coming through any affliction of life. If we are willing with God's presence to walk through, and not wait for the bridge over, when we emerge from the other side we can also know a little bit of the reality of resurrection. We will have experienced a new part of the essence of the victory of life, and, after all, resurrection is new life.

When I hear the melodic sound of "A Bridge Over Troubled Waters" I enjoy the tune, but as a Christian I cannot subscribe fully to the text. Yes, afflictions do come, but I do not cry out to my God for a bridge over; I humbly ask him for his presence so that we can travel a path through together.

> Sometimes on the mount where the sun shines so bright,
> God leads His dear children along;
> Sometimes in the valley in the darkest of night,
> God leads His dear children along.
> Some thro' the waters, some thro' the flood,
> Some thro' the fire, but all thro' the Blood;
> Some thro' great sorrow, but God gives a song,
> In the night season and all the day long.[2]

Notes

1. Mary Chase, *Harvey* (New York: Dramatist's Play Service, 1944), p. 49.

2. G. A. Young, "God Leads Us Along" (Kansas City: Lillenas Publishing Co., 1931).

5
I Made Peace with a Thorn

Life is always OK, except for something.

Remember that perfect time in your life? God was on his throne, and all seemed right with the world. You were alive with victory and new energy. How long did the celebration last? Soon came the clouds, the rain, and maybe even a storm. Your visit with the supermoment became a memory, and once again the mantle of mortal awareness settled in. *Such ecstasy is shortlived.*

My friend Gary Anderson was a prison chaplain. He describes prison inmates as "people trying to make-do with a limited life." Who is not in some way limited? Moses stuttered; Jacob limped; Jeremiah lived with a deficient self-image. We all have been halted in some degree by disease, accident, bad emotional models, personal inabilities, and/or missed opportunities. *All of us have our own limitations.*

Lincoln was freed from the burden of the great Civil War only to be cut down as he prepared to lead the nation into reconstruction. Sadat was murdered at the time he provided the viable bridge between the Jews and the Arabs in a seething conflict. Who has not endured the shock of having a dream or a goal shattered in a moment? *Life has its interruptions.*

Robert Taft, Adlai Stevenson, and Barry Goldwater all had more than a casual desire to be President of the United States. But each had to settle for "they also ran." *Great expectations are not always realized.*

So the trek from the cradle to the grave is never totally

complete, absolutely perfect, or lived out as planned, and many of the joys pass quickly away.

So what?

You can wait for life to be different, believing that your malady is just for a season. But "he who observes the wind will not sow; and he who regards the clouds will not reap" (Eccl. 11:4, RSV). Good advice!

You can settle into despair. Resignation from the human race is always possible. But that is a cowardly act of choice for self-damage or even self-destruction.

You can become a victim of self-pity. The population always includes some Jonahs who opt to sit under their gourd vines and pout because they are not in charge of the world or even true-life captains of their own souls.

You can deny reality. Woodrow Wilson was repeatedly asked and even begged to make peace with Henry Cabot Lodge to ensure that the Senate action regarding the League of Nations would be positive. Wilson, though, assumed that his executive power would triumph over Lodge's legislative strength. He lived in an illusion.

Over against the temptation of any of these options, listen to the great apostle tell his story:

> There was given me a thorn in the flesh, a messenger of Satan to buffet me—to keep me from exalting myself! Concerning this I entreated the Lord three times that it might depart from me. And He has said to me, "My grace is sufficient for you, for power is perfected in weakness." Most gladly, therefore, I would rather boast about my weaknesses, that the power of Christ may dwell in me. Therefore, I am well content with weaknesses, with insults, with distresses, with persecutions, with difficulties, for Christ's sake; for when I am weak, then I am strong (2 Cor. 12:7-10).

The apostle Paul has told us that his daily existence was always imperfect. Naturally he wished his affliction would disappear. But he had learned the reason for his malady and knew that God's grace was sufficient for that which he would bear.

Let's explore the passage.

Paul wrote to encourage the harmony and unity in the church of Corinth, but, even more, he bared his soul and let us in on how he was bearing his own personal affliction in life.

The Thorn Exists

The theories are numerous as to the nature of Paul's thorn. Some of the suggested speculations include poor eyesight, malaria, epilepsy, insomnia, migraine headaches, poor physical appearance, presence of evil thoughts, recurring grief and remorse over former hatred of Christ, and Paul's own persecution of Christians. A friend of mine has concluded that he believes that Paul was dissatisfied with his accomplishments, and this was his thorn in the flesh.

I believe the thorn was intensely personal to Paul. The reason he did not declare and identify his thorn plainly was due to its private nature. Besides, to label the malady more definitively would have been to run the risk of someone imitating him. Some facts are hidden away for our betterment.

But Paul did want us to know the characteristics of his affliction.

The thorn was painful. Pain is hurt in many descriptions.

The thorn was persistent. Paul readily advertised the constant and chronic nature of the pain.

The thorn could not be ignored. It buffeted Paul. Literally, the mysterious affliction beat at the servant of God like a repeated blow with a fist.

The thorn weakened Paul with a drawing, a depleting, a draining effect.

It is possible that each of us has a thorn or thorns. Paul is not the normal example for all of us. Only Jesus is the norm for each person. But Paul's message is given to us for aid in knowing that many of us will be afflicted. I am not saying that everyone has to have a thorn in the flesh. I am declaring that many will.

Your thorn is that which hurts you, limits you, that continuously troubles you, and/or will not go away. We are safe in saying the physical limits of deafness and blindness that affected Helen Keller were thorns. Periodic emotional exhaustion in the life of a prominent Midwestern pastor is a thorn. The consequences of past events that repeatedly disrupt life are a thorn. But jealousy, bitterness, broken relationships, or even overeating are not thorns. The grace of God and discipline can wipe those self-imposed sins out.

Can you put your finger where you hurt? Can you identify your own thorn? If so, how is it possible to live vigorously, even with the thorn?

The Thorn and a Normal Desire

Let's take a closer look at Paul's thorn. Thorns prick flesh. They aggravate, can fester, and become infected. They are a nuisance. But Paul did not use the term *thorn* as we think of the prickly points of a rose bush. His malady resembled a stake driven into the flesh. This heinous type of execution was carried out by impaling a prisoner or driving a stake into his body. Paul informs us the thorn was like a sharp stake that had been plunged into him. He continued by declaring his original and normal desire for God to remove the painful wound. Such response is natural, normal, and OK even for us. No normal person courts pain, but doctors remind us it is essential for normal and healthy, productive life.

The apostle Paul throughout his writings makes only a few references to prayer for his personal temporal needs. Usually he prays for spiritual edification of others and thanks God for his favors of grace. But here Paul's prayer is personally uplifting as we consider how to live with our own thorn or thorns. Paul knew he could take his pain to God. He bared his willingness to seek God. He knew that God would accept his personal needs. Besides, Paul knew God would respond. Therefore, we can rest assured that we can take our thorns before the Lord. This prayer is OK.

The Spiritual Reason for Thorns

Initially and repeatedly, Paul prayed for the thorn to be removed. But during these same prayer vigils he learned the reason for his affliction, how to bear the besetting trouble, and the fact that the nagging burden would continue to be with him.

Oh, what God can do with our prayers! He takes our feeble, tunnel-vision desires—and conditions them to his own will. Early in his life, Augustine, the great African bishop, wanted to leave his home in North Africa and go to Italy. His mother, Monica, fearing the journey to Rome would mean the ruin of his soul, prayed earnestly that he might be kept from sailing. Augustine, though, stowed away on a boat one night while his mother was on the shore. He had told her he was going on board the ship to visit a friend. When the morning dawned, the ship had sailed with him on board. His mother, brokenhearted and despondent, felt God had not answered her prayer. Truly her intercession had not been answered as to her first desire, but in substance the prayer was answered. She had been praying that her son might be restrained from going to Europe so that his soul might be saved. On the trip to Italy Augustine began step by step to move toward the great change that came over him one day in a garden in Milan when he heard the voice of God and found Christ as his Redeemer. Augustine later wrote, "But you did not do as she asked you then. Instead in the depth of your wisdom, you granted the wish that was closest to her heart. You did with me what she had always wanted you to do. . . . She did not know what joys you had in store for her because of my departure."[1]

Paul did not receive what he asked for, but God used his prayer for another purpose. The Scriptures clearly declare what God effected in Paul. The thorn was given "to me to keep me from exalting myself" (2 Cor. 12:7). Consult the Scriptures carefully here. This grievous trouble was given in the past and continued to be given to Paul. The gift lingered. Paul indicated that God was the giver, but we must be cautious in our interpretation here. The apostle was not saying that the giver, God, was the creator or originator of the gift. Rather God had given in that he took the existing trouble and made Paul's problem useful to his purpose and for Paul's good. Such is the nature of grace. The thorn was given to hold in check Paul's tendency to elation. Paul could easily become excited, especially by the unprecedented spiritual highs he received from God. But if such experiences were not tempered by the thorn, Paul might have concluded that he was special to God. Subsequently, the blessing of God's favor could have made the apostle proud. Pride is always selfish. Pride isolates a person. Pride declares independence, adequacy, and leaves no room for dependence on God. So we are safe in concluding that God used this thorn for Paul's good. This does not mean that God liked it. Our God was displeased with the rash and premeditated act of the sons of Jacob in selling their brother Joseph into slavery. Years later when Joseph rescued the family from famine and revealed himself to the same envious brothers, he advised, "Be not grieved, nor angry with yourselves, that ye sold me hither: for God did send me before you to preserve life" (Gen. 45:5, KJV). God did not smile as Bonhoeffer knelt in the snow moments before his execution in Germany, but we remember this German pastor as a twentieth-century example of faithful discipleship. Thorns do not please God, not even the thorns worn by his Son. But he does use the thorns. Thorns are remembered.

The Means of Bearing the Thorns

Because God is willing to use our inescapable thorns, he desires to make them bearable. There are always two ways to make a load more bearable. Either you lessen the weight or strengthen the bearer.

Paul's load did not change, but he discovered his own weakness in order to know God's strength. And that is the paradox of bearing the thorn.

Abraham Lincoln was a virile and vigorous product of the American frontier. His sense of self-worth was continually influenced by feelings of ugliness due to his gaunt and lanky appearance. His inclination to bouts of depression probably was related to his sense of inferiority. However, as a champion for the abolition of slavery he projected his inner strength and hardiness of character and compassion. A reporter for the *New York Evening Post* covering one of the 1858 Lincoln-Douglas debates observed, "In repose, I must confess that 'Long Abe's' appearance is not common, but stir him up and the fire of genius plays on every feature. Listening to him, calmly and unprejudiced, I was convinced that he has no superior as a stump speaker."[2] Apparently, Lincoln the presidential candidate possessed the innate potential to rise above any personal limitation in order to be strong for the rights of others.

Tragically this is not always the response. Some individuals, convinced they are shortchanged by life, allow their limitations to embitter them. Kaiser Wilhelm II was born with a withered and limp left arm. The affliction contributed to his sour disposition and advanced his tendency toward jealousy of any other strong-willed associate. He never made peace with the possibility that a German emperor could rule even as a cripple.[3] God can take our weaknesses and turn them into strength if we will allow him to do so.

Paul was never released from the load. But he did experience the daily sufficiency of God's grace to bear the load. God had a message for Paul. "My grace is sufficient for you" (2 Cor. 12:9). *Grace* is the New Testament word for God's adequacy. God's adequacy is sufficient for you and me. Sufficiency is the personal abiding power of God. God's adequacy is the personal abiding power of this presence.

Thorns are bearable through God's grace.

Notes

1. Augustine, *Confessions,* Book V, trans. by R.S. Pine-Coffin (London: Penguin, 1961), p. 101.

2. Carl Sandburg, *Abraham Lincoln: The Prairie Years and the War Years* (New York: Harcourt Brace and World, 1954), p. 139.

3. Irving Werstein, *The Many Faces of World War One* (New York: Julian Messner, 1963), p. 22.

6
I Can Live with Why!

Mystery is seldom immediately welcomed!

But life has mystery!

A child asks why. To his parents this nuisance question is a sign of the dawn of a worthy aspect of a healthy life.

A youth is disturbed by a barrage of new emotions and along the way wonders, *"Why me, here, now?"*

An adult experiences guilt for his own inadequacies. He worries over the economy, physical ailments, and possible disability and death and sighs, "I just don't know."

How do you respond?

"Do I have to?"

Yes! The alternative is crippling fear and limited progress. Disregard that loud bump in the night, and wonder and imagination fill the mind, the image of the "bogeyman" grows, and even panic can visit the soul.

Charles Goodyear experimented continuously in search of a means to harden rubber. If he had abandoned his search, our daily existence as a mobile people would be radically different. He would not give in to mystery.

Yes, we have to respond. Mystery is a primary subject in the curriculum of life. Works of fiction and adventure yarns satisfy our taste for wonder. Many have pondered the secrets of the Bermuda Triangle and speculated concerning the ships and planes swallowed up by the sea. The giant rocks of Stonehenge tell no stories of their origin, but many visitors to this English phenomenon harbor their own suspicions and surmises. The accounts of the Abominable Snowman and Big Foot intrigue us. UFO's were first reported in 1947, but forty-five hundred years ago the Chinese raised questions about wonders in the sky.

But mystery is much more personal than speculation into the realm of ethereal questions. When, how, where will I die? What will happen as I die? Will I know excruciating and even paralyzing pain? Will I slowly waste away? Will I still have a sense of vitality in my life but hear "we can do no more for him?" Will I lose my productivity and exist a long time idle? Will I be restricted to a spectator life-style and watch others in the daily pursuit of happiness while I grapple for existence and survival? Will I know the ache of hunger?

Or, did a virgin really give birth to the Son of God? Did Christ really provide atonement once and for all? Is God manifested in the Trinity? Why does God allow suffering? What will heaven be like?

Enough! This is all so heavy. I must quickly find a method, a scheme, a means by which I can make peace with some of the mystery I can neither evade nor avoid.

An old story in the Bible, the real-life drama of a human being well acquainted with and immersed in mystery, offers help. Listen to his story. Once in the land of Uz there lived a man whose name was Job. He was perfect, upright, feared God, and turned away from evil. He had seven sons and three daughters. His sustenance included seven thousand sheep, three thousand camels, five hundred yoke of oxen, five hundred she-asses, and a great household. Job was the greatest of all the children of the East.

This good and great family man was allowed to be tested. Caution! Remember God allowed him to be tested only to a point. God told Satan he might test Job; but, God said, "only do not put forth your hand on him" (1:12).

In a matter of hours, a succession of messengers rushed to tell Job of his sudden losses. The Sabeans took his oxen, asses, and the servants attending them. Fire from heaven burned up his sheep and other servants. The camels along with their attending servants were slain by the Chaldeans. "Great winds"—perhaps tornadoes or cyclones—shattered his oldest son's house, and all Job's sons and daughters were killed. Job grieved intensely. Through all the devastating tragedy Job did not sin and did not blame God.

Satan came to taunt him again. Once again God allowed Satan to test Job. But still God held on to Job by restricting Satan. "Only spare his life" (2:6). Boils covered Job's body, and he sat upon an ash pile scraping himself with a broken piece of pottery. His wife gazed in pity and exclaimed, "Do you still hold fast your integrity? Curse God and die!" (2:9). And, if this were not enough, three well-meaning friends came to comfort, console, and wait with their afflicted friend. Following a week of silence Job, Eliphaz, Bildad, and Zophar began to talk. Their conversation, exchange of ideas and convictions, plus the subsequent conclusion of the book offers some insight as to how we can make peace with our own mystery.

Job Welcomed His Own Questions

Listen to Job's self-interrogation.

"Shall we indeed accept good from God and not accept adversity?" (2:10).

"Why did I not die at birth,/. . ./Why did the knees receive me,/And why the breasts, that I should suck?" (3:11-12).

"What is my strength that I should wait?/And what is my end, that I should endure?" (6:11).

"When I lie down I say,/When shall I rise?" (7:4).

"What is man that Thou dost magnify him,/And that Thou art concerned about him,/That Thou dost examine him every morning,/And try him every moment?" (7:17).

"Wilt Thou never turn Thy gaze away from me,/Nor let me alone until I swallow my spittle?/Have I sinned? What have I done to Thee,/O watcher of men?/Why has thou set me as Thy target,/So that I am a burden to myself?" (7:19-20).

"But how can a man be in the right before God?" (9:2).

"How long will you torment me,/And crush me with words?" (19:2).

"Would He contend with me by the greatness of His power?" (23:6).

"But man dies and lies prostrate./Man expires and where is he?" (14:10).

"If a man dies, will he live again?" (14:14).

"But where can wisdom be found?/And where is the place of understanding?" (28:12).

These are not topics for rhetorical debate. Within the context of each expression resides fear, anger, hostility, anxiety, guilt, and an awesome sense of wonder. Job's questions announce feelings welling up out of the trauma of his own struggle and existence.

Listen to your questions. What is really bothering you or haunting you? What inescapable questions return over and over only to retreat again and again unanswered?

Why is my relative possessed by a habit that is torturing himself and hurting his family? Why did my mother or daddy leave emotional stains on me that daily drive me in unkind living? Why am I so shortchanged in talent and abilities in comparison to some people I know? Why cannot I relax and enjoy life? Why does the nightmare of past tragedy visit me again and again? Why was our family's joy and happiness cut short so tragically? Why did they tell me one day that I was healthy, only to warn me the next day of coming pain? Who do you know that lives with an absence of mystery?

We have to let the questions come. The great enemy of legitimate questions concerning our mysteries is fear, specifically the terror that we cannot provide the answer and the suspicion that God may be displeased with our questions. Both of these thoughts are guilt-laden.

The inability to answer kicks us right in the teeth. We hold tightly an insatiable desire for lordship over our own questions.

Besides, we are not really sure that God can or will accept us if we question him. Did anyone ever question God more than Job? Besides, how did the Bible come to be written? The Bible is the product of questions that were posed before God and answered through the inspiration of the Holy Spirit.

Our God not only receives our questions but also accepts us when we question him.

Job Held to What He Knew

Parallel to the struggle with his painful and inescapable questions was the fact that Job clung tenaciously to that which he believed. Listen to Job's convictions.

God is not intentionally punishing me. His friends had tried to tell him that he was living in iniquity. But Job replied, "Though He slay me,/I will hope in Him./Nevertheless, I will argue my ways before Him" (13:15).

I recognize my struggle. "Behold now, I have prepared my case;/I know that I will be vindicated" (13:18). But he continued, "How many are my iniquities and sins?/Make known to me my rebellion and my sin" (13:23).

I have self-worth. The friends had intimated to Job that he must repent and accept the judgment of God, but this righteous man declared, "What you know I also know./I am not inferior to you" (13:2).

Only God has ultimate understanding. "With Him are wisdom and might;/To Him belong counsel and understanding" (12:13).

God will be victorious. "And as for me I know that my Redeemer lives,/And at the last He will take His stand on the earth" (19:25). "I know that Thou canst do all things,/And that no purpose of Thine can be thwarted" (42:2).

God will sustain me. "For I know that thou will bring me to death/And to the house of meeting for all living" (30:23).

These convictions were Job's sustenance during his days of trial.

Ancient mariners moved into uncharted dark waters with

anxious questions. But sailing on they discovered new lands. We keep gradually pushing back the curtain of space wondering what we will find. Continuous courageous research has conquered polio and gives hope for the victory over cancer. But in all of these quests for answers the seekers could not neglect the basic convictions of the necessity of the struggle, the dependence on the work of others who also sought, and the beckoning call of risk. Within every mystery there are some basic convictions which must be held if one is to be sustained.

Examine your basic convictions. Do you really believe that by God's grace through faith you are saved? Is his grace really sufficient for you? Do you claim that whosoever believeth will not perish? Can you affirm "I can do all things through Christ"? Do you really believe that he will lead you through the valley and the shadow of death? Can you testify to the fact that nothing can separate you from God? What convictions sustain you in the midst of trial?

Job Discovered Only God Can Handle Most Mysteries

Discussion and debate dominate the Book of Job. A sorrowing man and his three friends faced suffering, the questions of sin, and the possible need of repentance amid pain. All along, though, God was patiently waiting with intimate interest and observing the whole scenario. Then sometime following the discussion Job experienced a new dimension of God. Remember Job had challenged the Lord. "Then call, and I will answer;/Or let me speak, then reply to me" (13:22). In another discourse he cried, "Let me know why Thou dost contend with me" (10:2). All along the struggle Job inferred that he had an indisputable word on the action and ways of God. He was not hesitant to call upon God at his own choice and time.

And then, at his own chosen moment, God spoke. Allow *The Living Bible* to guide us at this point.

Then the Lord answered Job out of the whirlwind and said:

Why are you using your ignorance to deny my providence? Now get ready to fight, for I am going to demand some answers from you, and you must reply. Where were you when I laid the foundations of the earth? Tell me if you know so much. (38:2-4)

Have you ever once commanded the morning to appear and caused the dawn to rise in the east? (38:12)

Has the rain a father? Where does dew come from? Who is the mother of the ice and frost? (38:28-29)

Who gives intuition and instinct? Who is wise enough to number all the clouds? Who can tilt the water jars of heaven when everything is dust and clouds? (38:36-38)

Do you know how mountain goats give birth? (39:1)

Who makes the wild donkeys wild? (39:5)

Have you given the horse strength or clothed his neck with a quivering mane? (39:19)

Can you catch [an alligator] with a hook and line? Or put a noose around his tongue? (41:1-2)

In all of these questions God was challenging Job to take a hard look at his own knowledge and understanding. But even more, God was reminding Job of his own humanity, mortality, and lack of understanding. God was cutting away at Job's own concept of himself. God cut him down to human size.

What will God choose to teach you about yourself during the time of your own mystery?

George Washington Carver devoutly believed that a personal relationship to the Creator of all things was the only foundation to live the abundant life and the only atmosphere in which to wrestle with these pressing questions. He used a little story to relate this conviction.

I asked the Great Creator what the universe was made for.

"Ask for something more in keeping with that little mind of yours," he replied.

"What was man made for?"

"Little man, you still want to know too much; cut down the extent of your request and improve the intent."

Then I told the Creator I wanted to know all about the peanut. He replied that my mind was too small to know all about the peanut, but he said he would give me a handful of peanuts. Then God said, "Behold I have given you every herb bearing seed, which is upon the face of the earth. To you it shall be for meat. . . . I have given every green herb for meat and it was so."

I carried the peanuts into my laboratory and the Creator told me to take them apart and resolve them into the elements. With such knowledge as I had of chemistry and physics I set to work to take them apart. There, I had the parts of the peanut all spread out before me. I looked at Him and He looked at me and said, "Now you know what the peanut is."

"Why did you make the peanut?"

The Creator said, "I have given you three laws; namely, compatibility, temperature and pressure. All you have to do is take the constituents and put them together, observing these laws, and I will show you why I made the peanut."[1]

Wise is the man who allows God in the midst of his own mystery to bring him down to his own size.

Job Refused to Allow Mystery to Consume Him

Job chose not to react with bitterness and despair.

The Bible indicates that he reached out to others. Early in the book there is evidence of broken relationships existing between Job and members of his own family and his friends.

He has removed my brothers far from me,
And my acquaintances are completely estranged from me.
My relatives have failed,
And my intimate friends have forgotten me.
Those who live in my house and my maids consider me a stranger.
I am a foreigner in their sight.
I call to my servant but he does not answer.
My breath is offensive to my wife,
And I am loathsome to my own brothers.
Even young children despise me;
I rise up and they speak against me.

All my associates abhor me,
And those I love have turned against me (19:13-20)

While these words reflect Job's feelings during his suffering, nevertheless, following his agony new ties and relationships had to be formed.

In the final chapter of the book we discover a beautiful scene describing his brothers, sisters, and acquaintances coming together to eat with him in his house. The Bible says they comforted him in the midst of all his affliction.

Also the Scriptures indicate that Job prayed for his friends (see 42:10). This is evidence that he lost his preoccupation with himself and reached out to others even in the midst of his own continuing mystery. Such scriptural lessons challenge us not to be bogged down in our own mysteries and miss the opportunity of healing relationships with other people as well as continuing to reach out to others.

In addition, Job resumed living. He still had his great losses and his bodily pain, but he moved back into the mainstream of life. The final picture of Job is a portrait of prosperity. However, the Bible is not trying to say that the man was made more prosperous because he went through the ordeal. Instead the picture reflects a man resuming the vitality of life and seeking to fill the void of his own losses. Many times, mystery brings to us a new acquaintance with loss. But we have to seek to fill the voids that are caused by mystery.

John Donne once said, "Mysteries in souls do grow." But we do not have to end this chapter with that statement. That is, from the Christian perspective, only an admission of mystery. But our Christ offers us much more. One day Jesus gathered his disciples around him. They were his intimate share group. He loved them, and he shared himself continually with them. Over and over again they came with questions. On that occasion in response to their questions he said, "To you it has been granted to know the mysteries of the kingdom of heaven" (Matt. 13:11). This message can sustain us in the midst of our mysteries. Through our intimate relationship with Christ we can know the great mysteries of the kingdom, and these spiritual realities can sustain us.

Note

1. Rackham Holt, *George Washington Carver, An American Biography* (Garden City, New York: Doubleday Doran & Co., 1943), pp. 226-227. Used by permission.

7

If I Am Ready to Die,
I'm Ready to Live

Mike Taylor was dying.

He had accepted his death and was willing to narrate the final stage of his earthly pilgrimage. In an article describing his bout with leukemia he made two intriguing statements: one was quite alarming; the other was indeed refreshing.

First, Mike announced, "It's un-American to die."[1] I was shocked but more angered at his pronouncement. For over two centuries a dynamic quality of the American heritage has been our willingness to sacrifice life for the cause of freedom. How dare he utter such unpatriotic nonsense?

Actually he was confronting me with inescapable truth. Americans do shun death. We do not like to keep company with the thought of our own personal finality.

As I reflected on my existential encounter in confronting my own demise I recognized both a tug and a pull. I was pulled toward the subject of death with a compelling curiosity; yet simultaneously I felt a tug away as the temptation to flee scored a quick victory over the weakening desire to stay and think about death. Out of this strange ambivalence I was encountering the fact that death was the ultimate threat to my existence. So, yes, realistically, it is un-American to die. We of the generation of the macho look and the alluring quest for the heroes we vicariously imitate do not welcome the "fault" of dying.

But Mike's second statement refreshed me. "I feared I would feel like a dead man walking among the living. Now that I have been forced to deal with death, I feel many times like the living walking among the dead."[2] You and I might reflect and say, "Oh, yes, that's easy for him to say. He is terminal." But so are we; we each entered into the terminal state the very moment of our own conception. So that argument for shunning death goes out the window.

Mike Taylor shared much more in his testimony forecasting his own forthcoming death. Each sentence was a witness to honesty, courage, and faith. However, as I reflected on the entire article I realized that he was saying to me, "I am ready to die, and out of the resolve I have become ready to live." Such a personal message I could not escape.

I trust quite sincerely that death for me is in the distant future. But in the time dimension of the immediate now I ponder the ongoing tension, "Am I so ready to die that I am ready to live?"

How does a person prepare to die that he might be prepared to live?

Our best approach in this inescapable pursuit is to encounter Jesus' readiness to die. If we look at our Lord only from the standpoint of the divine dimension we will miss the human Savior giving us the good news of readiness to face death, which in turn, makes us ready to live. This is our quest: to find in the life of Christ how we can become ready to die that we might be ready to live.

I Am Ready to Die and Live If I Am Convinced that God's Life Purpose for Me Is Being Realized

According to Matthew's Gospel Jesus tested his followers at Caesarea Philippi. He asked each of them to declare his identity. Peter quickly accepted the challenge and affirmed "Thou art the Christ, the Son of the Living God" (16:16). Following their conversation the Bible says that "From that time Jesus Christ began to show His disciples that He must go to Jerusalem, and suffer many things from the elders and chief priests and scribes, and be killed, and be raised up on the third day" (16:21). But what prompted Jesus to speak of his death at this opportune time? Peter's confession gave Jesus the evidence that his purpose was being realized. Someone by faith had seen him for what he was and who he was. The crucial value here for us lies in the reality that recognition of God's purpose in our lives defeats futility. Each of us harbors a hope that our individual life on earth has made a difference. Nothing could create despondency more than to come to the end of life with the unresolved question, "Why was I here?" The impotence of our own existence is removed when we know we have a God-given purpose.

Realized purpose in life provides the satisfaction and celebration of personal worth. In the Caesarea Philippi event Jesus was released to face the future in a new way. He had been actively and aggressively pursuing his purpose, and Peter's confession equipped him with a readiness for whatever he would encounter. Once we discover God's purpose for our lives and become involved in pursuing God's intention, God may possibly break in at some point and say, "You are fulfilling my why for you." Thus recognition of personal purpose gives us release. We realize that we are not here by some cosmic explosion or accident, but we are worth something and God intended for us to be here.

An English professor once gave his class an unusual assignment: "Prepare for your own funeral." Each pupil was to visit a funeral home, select a casket, make all the arrangements, and even write out his own obituary. The teacher later commented that most of the obituaries revealed that the majority of the students felt they had wasted their lives. The person who lives feeling such remorse is a person who is neither ready to live nor ready to die. There is great dissatisfaction in that person. The inability to find purpose gives an annoying existence rather than a sense of satisfaction. He is somewhat like the child who went to school the first day and along the way lost his birth certificate. He traveled the last part of the road in fear. Arriving at the school he told the teacher, "I lost my excuse for being born."

When a person finds his purpose and is in the process of pursuing that purpose he has a reason both to live and he has discovered a readiness for dying.

I Am Ready to Die and Live If I Have Christ's View of Death

How do you really view your own death?

Do you fear the grim reaper?

Do you envision the coming of a pale horse?

Possibly you harbor the ambivalence of Job who declared, "Man dies and lies prostrate. Man expires and where is he?" Only moments later he asked "If a man dies, will he live again?" (14:10,14).

Other Scriptures offer more consistency. Moses, Jeremiah, Daniel, Stephen, David, and Paul were unanimous in labeling death as sleep. But there is even more assurance of death as sleep in Jesus' loving act of raising Lazarus from the dead. Jesus, ready to make the trip to Bethany, said to his disciples, "Our friend Lazarus has fallen asleep; but I go, that I may awaken him out of sleep" (John 11:11). Apparently the followers had more than a curious interest in Jesus' announcement. They considered sleep and waking up as normal sequence. Why would their Master need to be present to awaken his friend? Jesus used their interest as a teachable moment to offer them a new perspective on death, as unique sleep from which only he could awaken the sleeper. Sleep is meant to be pleasant, relaxing, and bring strength and nurture to the body. But, moreover, remember that you awaken from sleep. Sleep in the Scripture is presented as a period of quietness and relaxation from which the sleeper awakens. The despair of the final end is removed, and death becomes less the ultimate threat as we think of our own death as sleep from which he will personally awaken us.

I Am Ready to Die and Live When I Admit My Struggle to Live on Is Inevitable

Strange?

I am expressing the great inescapable human ambivalence. I am talking of the will to live that comes in contest and battle with my readiness to die. We never escape this dynamic tension.

Go into Gethsemane. Listen to Jesus' conversational prayer with the Father. The human desire is uttered first. "My Father, if it is possible, let this cup pass from Me." Immediately the divine understanding conflicts with the human desire. "Yet not as I will, but as Thou wilt" (Matt. 26:39). We know from the events of his life following those moments at Gethsemane that he completely accepted the will of the Father and went on to the cross for our redemption. We cannot do as he did. We, not being Christ, cannot so accept. We struggle. We clutch. We hold on. Our resignation and surrender are never as complete as his. Even Paul never experienced this resolve as totally as Christ did: "For to me, to live is Christ, and to die is gain. . . . But I am hard-pressed from both directions, having the desire to depart and be with Christ, for that is very much better; yet to remain on in the flesh is more necessary for your sake" (Phil. 1:21,23). Paul was writing from some jail to his beloved Philippians. And he realized his time of earthly departure was close at hand. Nevertheless, he continued to admit his struggle.

We must accept the fact that we will keep struggling to live—even though we recognize that we must be ready to die. Our readiness to die, even to the moment of death, will struggle with the God-given will to live.

I Am Ready to Die and Live When I Remember that God Goes Through Death with Me

The foremost fear of death is the awesome reality that I will die alone, and that there is no report as to what to expect.

Death is the single undeniable and inescapable experience each person must encounter totally alone. A relative, friend, physician, pastor, or mere acquaintance can abide with us only up to the actual moment of death. Death is a solitary act and a solo journey. And while we struggle to live on we will be acted upon by a power, the last enemy whose force we cannot repel or defeat. This is comparable to the helpless feeling parents experience as their child is taken to surgery while they wait outside the door in an abyss of alienation and frustration. But our comfort as believers rises as we remember that a thief hanging on a cross by Jesus' side asked, "Jesus, remember me." And Jesus immediately responded, "Today . . . you shall be with Me in Paradise" (Luke 23:43). Our Lord in compassion was indicating to this vile and adjudged evil man that he would be with him. There is absolutely nothing that our God is not willing to go through with us, even death. His is the only presence we need. For the Christian, death will be a moment of new introduction and the first full meeting with Christ. Before death we know our Lord only in part, for we are limited by our own human frailties and sins. But going through the valley and the shadow we meet, literally face to face, the one who desires to never leave us comfortless.

I Am Ready to Die and Live When I Believe in the Resurrection

Jesus never talked about his death unless he also mentioned the resurrection. What comfort! What assurance! Oh, the joy of the promise of hope!

The risen Christ declared victory over death. His resurrection is constantly a clear signal that death is not the ultimate end. The climactic triumph reemphasized his own words, "He is not the God of the dead but of the living" (Matt. 22:32). For a Christian, in a real sense there is no such thing as final death to God. Death is transition. Human death is God's means by which we move from this dimension of living into a greater dimension of life with him.

One day the apostle Paul wrote a letter to a young man named Timothy. Paul recognized his life on earth was about to close. To Timothy he said:

> The time of my departure has come. I have fought the good fight, I have finished the course, I have kept the faith; in the future there is laid up for me the crown of righteousness, which the Lord, the righteous Judge, will award to me on that day; and not only to me, but also to all who have loved His appearing (2 Tim. 4:6-8).

The old missionary was expressing a sense of satisfaction and joy in living coupled with the readiness to accept the transition, the passing over into the full presence of Christ.

He was prepared to die, for he had been prepared by Christ to live.

Notes

1. Mike Taylor, "Death Says No, Death Says Yes," in *The Baptist Program*, June 1980.
2. Ibid.

II
Receiving God's Grace

8
I Am What I Am
by the Grace of God

A popular farm magazine once featured a cartoon entitled "Hambone." The character's popularity made his name a household word, and his wit and wisdom were readily quoted by farmers, townsfolk, and city dwellers alike. Hambone once commented, "I am what I am because I am what I am."

One fresh and warm spring morning I bounced on to an elevator in a Nashville hospital. The only other rider was a young lady. She, dressed in white, carrying a tray of laboratory vials, wore a facial expression advertising despair. Probably caught up in my delight in the spring weather and feeling the need to offer cheer, I commented, "You must be one of those people who take blood." She raised her head, looked straight at me, and flatly said, "I am anything they want me to be."

The apostle Paul in a crescendo moment of willful self-exposure told his Corinthian friends, "by the grace of God I am what I am" (1 Cor. 15:10).

Such diverse commentary represents the three real choices I can make as to who I am and who I become.

Who am I—the real me—in this plastic age? Identity, personal being is the challenging quest of multitudes today. Folk, from adolescents to senior adults, healthy and sick, wealthy and impoverished, secure and lonely, active and lazy, all cry, "I am . . . " and long to fill in the blank.

I am . . . the yield of my conglomerate genes and chromosomes in biological arrangement.

I am . . . the nurture of parents mixed with freedom and authority.

I am . . . expresses my education: both formal, coincidental, and accidental.

I am . . . includes my birth and personal looks.

I am . . . the point in life now and all that brought me up to now.

I am . . . is the existential quiz to know what makes me tick, react, respond, think, and feel.

I am . . . the sum of my roles—parent, husband, pastor, writer, citizen.

I am . . . me, the human being, naked and exposed, wraps pushed aside to reveal another—*imago dei*.

I am . . . is the ongoing, ever-moving quest for life's goals pursued with a mirror in hand lest I lose touch with me.

Neither testimony nor analysis must ever camouflage my three primary choices. Who I am is either a bad and feeble effort to make myself, the sad result of surrender of my being to the exploits of others, or a person after his likeness, by grace.

Self-Made Me

Admittedly, I can take the stuff called me and attempt to make myself, irrespective of other influences. Because this appeals to my self-sufficiency, I must take a hard look at a self-made man before I begin.

Matthew, Mark, and Luke all include the story of the man who came to Jesus and asked "what shall I do to inherit eternal life?" (Luke 18:18). At first glance I applaud and commend him. But when I join the three Gospel narratives and form his composite picture I view the tragedy of a self-made man. He carries the label rich young ruler or, more descriptively, wealthy youthful man of authority. He seems drawn to Jesus and opens the discussion with condescending flattery bordering on arrogance. "What shall I do?" The question betrayed the very security he advertised. He was dissatisfied and knew something was missing. Yet he appeared confident and convinced that if the proper action were outlined for him he would fulfill the requirements to possess eternal life.

If earlier he had overheard Jesus' message on receiving the kingdom as a child (Mark 10:13-16), the man might have concluded the requirements for adults were certainly more demanding.

Jesus' review of the Commandments was immediately met with the self-reliant man's claim to moral perfection. He had deceived himself to the point of believing all his personal relationships were OK.

Still Jesus did not give up. Christ confronted the impulsive man with the tragic flaw in his own being. "One thing you still lack: sell all that you possess, and distribute it to the poor, and you shall have treasure in heaven; and come, follow Me" (Luke 18:22).

Mark who first wrote this story gives us the best description of his response: "but at these words his face fell, and he went away grieved, for he was one who owned much property" (Mark 10:22).

What's wrong here?

A man has discovered what he had become. Jesus revealed to him that he was what he had produced. He had lived ignorant of who he was becoming. He owned much, but in the obsession to possess he had become bound. His grief was deep and confining. Grief is always an expression of separation. The rich young ruler—the self-made man—was divided between his desire for eternal life and his inability to turn loose that which possessed him.

He is the classic New Testament self-made man, the only man who, without question, rejected Jesus' personal invitation to follow him. The man he had been busy making could not leave to follow Jesus.

Instead he went away.

—Unable to praise God for giving him a new beginning. He was, in Isaiah's terms, as clay that questioned the potter (Isa. 45). And he had forgotten that the potter had a claim on his life (Rom. 9:21).

—Into his own fashioned solitude to draw his circle around himself and maybe to muse over his missed chance to break out of himself.

—To continue his great sin of self-idolatry and wallow on his bed of narcissistic discomfort.

In one of his books C. Roy Angell tells the story of a man who prided himself on being self-made. One evening he went to visit a business associate in his home. Before the friend came into the living room his little girl came in. She said to the caller, "My daddy says you are a self-made man. Why did you make yourself that way?" At first the man was puzzled by the child's question. Later that evening he began to think again of the question and looked at himself in the mirror. He noticed that his clothes were wrinkled, actually splotched with food stains, his shoes were unpolished, and his general appearance suffered with lack of care. He reflected on his daily routine and realized that he was obsessed with his need to succeed. All in all, the child's question began to haunt him concerning the product that he had manufactured of himself.

They Made Me

Yes! Tragically, many folks allow other folks to fashion their being.

Remember Pilate? This career politician, who was perhaps about Jesus' age, arrived in Judea aware that the Jews were a thorn in the Roman flesh. The young procurator was aware that his success in the assignment could endear him to Caesar. Evidently he was unprepared to face the power of Caiaphas and shortly incurred the high priests' wrath because of three critical mistakes. On his initial visit to the Holy City Pilate allowed the soldiers to bear standards carrying the bust of Caesar. The image of the emperor-god was greatly offensive to the Jews. Pilate initiated the construction of an aqueduct with good intentions but erred in attempting to finance the water system with Temple money. A further blunder was to permit the soldiers to use shields embossed with the emperor's name. Once again the emperor-god insignia angered the Jewish rank and file.

By now the emperor had warned Pilate not to incite the Jews and maintain the Pax Romana. One more incident could destroy his career and even himself. Thus, by the time Jesus appeared before the governor, his excellency was running scared. Face to face with the Christ, Pilate's real being surfaced.

The Scripture tells the story.

They led him [Jesus] away, and delivered Him up to Pilate. (Mark 15:1b)

Pilate therefore said to them, "Take Him yourselves, and judge Him according to your law." The Jews said to him, "We are not permitted to put anyone to death." (John 18:31)

Pilate therefore entered again into the Praetorium, and summoned Jesus, and said to Him, "Are you the King of the Jews?" Jesus answered, "Are you saying this on your own initiative, or did others tell you about Me?" Pilate answered "I am not a Jew, am I? Your own nation and the chief priests delivered You up to me; what have You done?" (John 18:33-35)

And when he had said this he [Pilate] went out again to the Jews, and said to them "I find no guilt in Him." (John 18:38b)

And when he [Pilate] learned that He belonged to Herod's jurisdiction, he sent Him to Herod, who himself also was in Jerusalem at that time. (Luke 23:7)

And Herod with his soldiers, after treating Him [Jesus] with contempt and mocking Him, dressed Him in a gorgeous robe and sent Him back to Pilate. (Luke 23:11)

And Pilate summoned the chief priests and the rulers and the people, and said to them, "You brought this man to me as one who incites the people to rebellion, and behold, having examined Him before you, I have found no guilt in this man regarding the charges which you make against Him." (Luke 23:13-14)

And while he was sitting on the judgment seat, his wife sent to him, saying, "Have nothing to do with that righteous Man; for last night I suffered greatly in a dream because of Him." But the chief priests and the elders persuaded the multitudes to ask for Barabbas and to put Jesus to death. But the governor answered and said to them, "Which of the two do you want me to release for you?" And they said, "Barabbas." (Matt. 27:19-21)

And Pilate came out again, and said to them, "Behold I am bringing Him out to you, that you know that I find no guilt in Him." Jesus therefore came out, wearing a crown of thorns and the purple robe. And Pilate said to them, "Behold the Man!" When therefore the chief priests and the officers saw Him they cried out, saying, "Crucify! crucify!" Pilate said to them, "Take Him yourselves, and crucify Him, for I find no guilt in Him." The Jews answered him, "We have a law, and by that law He ought to die because He made Himself out to be the Son of God." When Pilate therefore heard this statement he was the more afraid; and he entered into the Praetorium again, and said to Jesus, "Where are You from?" But Jesus gave him no answer. Pilate therefore said to Him, "You do not speak to me? Do You not know that I have the authority to release You, and I have the authority to crucify You?" Jesus answered, "You would have no authority over Me, unless it had been given to you from above; for this reason he who delivered me up to you has the greater sin." As a result of this Pilate made efforts to release Him, but the Jews cried out saying, "If you release this man you are no friend of Caesar; everyone who makes himself out to be a king opposes Caesar." (John 19:4-12)

The attempt to pawn the task off on Herod failed. Pilate had appealed to tradition, but the Jewish mob could not be satisfied with Jesus receiving holiday clemency. Even the offer to compromise—flog Jesus and release him—was ineffective.

Pilate did not relish condemning and executing Jesus. Quite the contrary, Jesus intrigued him. Besides, the governor knew the Jews were exploiting and manipulating him. A heavy and deepening shadow of public opinion was gaining control. We cannot excuse the Roman ruler due to prevailing conditions. He had become a victim of the need to please the populace, to harmonize with the local clientele. The situation, namely the power of the people, conditioned the man. His anxiety intensified. His vocation and his life was threatened. The man, symbol of mighty Rome, representative of the emperor, succumbed to fear engendered by the press of the people.

> And when Pilate saw that he was accomplishing nothing, but rather that a riot was starting, he took water and washed his hands in front of the multitude, saying, "I am innocent of this Man's blood; see to that yourselves." And all the people answered and said, "His blood be on us and on our children." Then he [Pilate] released Barabbas for them; but after having Jesus scourged he delivered Him to be crucified." (Matt. 27:24-26)

Pilate was a "they-made man" at his worst. He could not take a stand for Christ.

Grace Made Me

Paul is the best example. "By the grace of God I am what I am" (1 Cor. 15:10).

Years earlier he had breathed "threats and murder against the disciples of the Lord" (Acts 9:1) and "persecuted this Way to the death, binding and putting both men and women into prisons" (Acts 22:4). The zealot admitted, "And when the blood of Thy witness Stephen was being shed, I also was standing by approving, and watching out for the cloaks of those who were slaying him" (Acts 22:20). "And as I punished them often in all the synagogues, I tried to force them to blaspheme; and being furiously enraged at them, I kept pursuing them even to foreign cities" (Acts 26:11).

Then, Paul was called by the grace of God (Gal. 1:15). God summoned him through his presence, but not initially to be an apostle or missionary. More basic, Christ chose the man hostile to the name of Jesus to be himself, to be Paul. The first call from God always includes the opportunity to be real, to surrender all we make of ourselves and all we allow other folk to make of us. The change only began as Christ became real to the persecutor of Christians.

Paul had been selected to preach to the Gentiles. But he did not immediately pursue this ministry. He did not even hasten to Jerusalem to identify with the other apostles. Rather, "I went away to Arabia'' (Gal. 1:17). Why? By his own choice and wooed by God's Spirit, the new disciple was led away into the presence of God as was Moses in Midian, Jacob at Peniel, the prodigal beside the hog pen—that is grace. With only himself on his hands Paul began his self-discovery through the power of grace. Grace, the offering of God's redeeming presence, showed him both the boldness and compassion he must possess. Through grace he experienced the vitality and patience to balance his life. By grace he grasped both the urgency and reserve that had to control his ministry. Only then could Paul return to begin his public ministry, a life of servanthood lived out in grace; for Paul later would testify to being conducted along by His grace (see 2 Cor. 1:12).

Again, what is grace?

According to my wife, Lynn, "Grace is the sum total of all that God gives me that I do not deserve that enables me to be me, and makes me want to be me. I can run the risk of being me because of his grace."

We live amid the rushing traffic of other people. Unlike passing cars, we touch; and, inevitably, we are influenced. I follow my dreams and hopes and expend my own energy in the pursuit of success, public acclaim, and other causes I do not even see. Such is inescapable.

Yet I, in a world with others and often unconscious of my desire to make myself, must keep on affirming: I can be what I am supposed to be—only by God's grace.

9
Jesus Broke a Trail That I May Follow

Some years ago, one of our dogs "blessed" the family with a new litter of puppies. They were unexpected, to say the least. Individually, the pups had little, if any, uniqueness. They were the same color. They made similar sounds. They even smelled the same. In fact, about all I could determine was that each dog was growing. Periodically, as I checked on them, they each were larger in size.

We share a variety of personal information with our peer group, church family, or circle of friends. We often, in turn, become well acquainted with their likes, dislikes, habits, and feelings. But in all the accumulated knowledge of our acquaintances, have we noticed if they are growing in their human potential and Christlikeness?

Jesus' life prior to age twelve is shrouded in much mystery. We can only speculate concerning those years of silence; probably the twelve years were quite normal. As a child he learned obedience to authority. He began to walk, talk, use his muscles, and observe his surroundings. He probably enjoyed a very simple and arduous home life, possibly broken only by the weekly event of sabbath worship. From his later ministry we can guess that he was a keen observer of nature, seeing the lilies, birds, sheep, and foxes. Aside from suppositions as these, one fact is clear: he was growing. The only authentic fact of Jesus' life during this time verified by Scripture is Luke's commentary that: "The Child continued to grow and became strong, increasing in wisdom; and the grace of God was upon Him" (Luke 2:40).

The principle of growth magnified his early life. The serious

Christian never has a choice concerning growth. Either one grows, or one gradually wastes one's potential and gifts. Persons who want to be Christian and have no desire to mature are persons content to have their souls saved but waste their lives. Thus, I ask the question, dare we encounter Christ's principle of growth?

The Principle of Growth

Following his twelfth birthday Jesus attended the Temple services and festivities in Jerusalem with his family. The Jerusalem visit presents the initial picture of Jesus as the pupil Christ. He apparently realized that Jewish religion had become sterile and hollow. The Temple encounter with the elders clues us in to the reality that his preparation for his adult ministry began quite early. Luke's summary of the next eighteen years is again the only scriptural reference encompassing a long period of Jesus' life. We can well conclude Luke's desire was to record the most important feature of Jesus' early life. As John had captured the essence of the incarnation in the expression "the Word became flesh" (John 1:14), so Luke characterized Jesus' development as "increasing in wisdom and stature, and in favor with God and men" (Luke 2:52). The descriptive word for his growth is often translated *increase* or *advance*. Actually the word picture summarizes the activity of Christ's life during that time. The term describes the work of a group of men who are cutting down trees and clearing away brush to provide a road upon which people can later travel. A good English translation of what was happening during that formative period is to say that Jesus was pioneering.

A native of Reading, Pennsylvania, with little schooling became a scholar in the woods of mid-America, and the five-foot-nine-inch strong man led settlers into the Kentucky wilderness. Daniel Boone remains a giant of the American pioneering effort.

During the nineteenth century a Georgia physician reputedly became the first doctor in the United States to perform surgery using ether as an anesthetic, and Crawford W. Long's name is listed as a pioneer in medical science.

A German scientist emigrated to the United States in the 1930s as the Nazi political machine stifled life in his fatherland. But Albert Einstein continued his pioneering study in the relation of mass and energy, and the transplanted American pioneer revolutionized scientific principles.

Two men from earth, Neil A. Armstrong and Edwin E. Aldrin, Jr., first set foot on the moon July 20, 1969, inaugurating a whole new dimension in space pioneering.

A most self-reliant widow moved her children into Fort Harrod in the American wilderness, and Ann Lindsay proved that a woman could pioneer in establishing home life in primitive conditions.

All were different pioneers, part of the stuff that made this nation. They were people willing to move into the unknown. But such a pioneering spirit is not native only to the American nation. Actually, it dates back at least to Asian ancient history as "By faith Abraham, when he was called, . . . he went out, not knowing where he was going" (Heb. 11:8). Then again, it is portrayed in the Judean wilderness in the forerunner of Jesus Christ, John the Baptist. But for the Christian, the pioneering principle is much more dynamic in Christ's example.

Why is the pioneering idea so important for us? Is it only an insatiable desire to know what is over the hill or around the next bend? I think not. The pioneering growth model of Jesus Christ is part of God's expectation. Yes, God is displeased when we break his Ten Commandments and violate his royal law of love. But our God is also never happy with our static living. God created trees, grass, cows, horses, dogs, and cats, and they grow by natural law. This is normal and natural, but a person, aside from physical growth, must choose his mental, emotional, and spiritual maturity. We make this choice.

Furthermore, growth in the Christ example is essential lest we neglect the Christian responsibility of maturity. The world today needs pioneering Christians to move into new frontiers. Let me stress the immediacy of the need. As a teenager I used to help my father in his blacksmith shop. One of my jobs was to be a striker (not in the common use of the term today). Dad would bring a piece of red-hot iron out of the forge and lay it on the anvil for me to hit or strike with a hammer. I learned very quickly that you have to strike when the iron is hot. Today the time is right: the iron is hot for the work and ministry of the church. But more effective ministry will require personal pioneering.

The pioneering venture requires new appreciation and acceptance of a beautiful, dynamic, and challenging word—*change*. Each of the American pioneers I have mentioned, the patriarch Abraham, as well as our Savior Jesus Christ, all had one basic feature in common as pioneers. They accepted change in their own lives and effected change in other lives.

Change is not a term or process to deify or worship. Change is a course of action that requires caution, patience, and much prayer. Change, though, is basic to understanding the gospel. The fundamental idea of gospel redemption is a life being changed. A church should effect some healthy, wholesome change in its community. A Christian is called to grow and change into Christlikeness. There are phenomenal possibilities for each of us if we allow the potential of the pioneering example of Christ to come into our individual lives.

Looking further into the pioneering example of Christ we discover the nature of vibrant growth. Growth is realizing that here I am and there I can be and in that atmosphere pursuing an envisioned destiny. Growth is Jesus saying, "you are Simon, but you can be called Peter" (see Matt. 16:18). Growth is Jesus challenging us to be complete. The connotation of that term carries the idea that we are to ripen. Some of us have been pulled green. Growth is realizing and recognizing our potential; growth is becoming alive to self with God's help.

Such growth must be intentional. In an age of automation and instant replay it is easy to forget growth. Remember, we do not have an automatic pilot that follows a set course. Business technology today too often sets the pace for us, and we are tempted to fall in and become apathetic to intentional growth. We have to make growth happen. Jesus' growth came in spite of difficulties, not through their absence. No life knew more problems and obstacles than the life of our Lord. Even in the presence of constant tension he maintained a spirit of discipline joined with arduous efforts and an attitude that was never passive, apathetic, or slothful. He kept moving on.

The Growth Dimension

Luke presents the dimensions of Jesus' growth in four parts. Each represents an aspect of the Nazarene's total life. Thus the physician-writer was saying that Jesus pioneered in all areas of his life.

First, he grew in wisdom.—As you compare verses 40 and 52 of Luke 2 you find that from birth up to age twelve Jesus was primarily growing physically. His pilgrimage from age twelve to age thirty was governed by the priorities of his mental growth. During that period of maturation he was encountering adolescence and early adulthood, the time when a person begins to meet the perplexing questions about life. This was a noble era when his mind began to surge forth to be free from rote behavior and he began to experiment with his own freedom. Christ was being exposed to his world, and he was formulating his own philosophy of life. In a real sense Jesus was moving through his early years trying to hew out meaning from life. Tragedy is the label that must be placed upon anyone who has matured physically and missed the agony of having to come alive to himself. Jesus faced life's difficulties and sought answers—literally hacking out the way of life and surpassing the average education of his time and gaining the knowledge of divine truth. William James of Harvard once said that the average person used 10 percent of his mental capacity. Jesus used much more.

Second, the Jewish lad grew in stature.—So many of the

paintings of Jesus look effeminate. Jesus is crowned with a halo, and his eyes are docile and even dazed. Most of these paintings represent failures to see Jesus as human. A few years ago Richard and Frances Hook began depicting Christ in an unprecedented reality. They rebelled against the previous characterizations of Jesus. In their art offering, which conceptualized Jesus as infant, lad, and mature man, the virile and masculine features of the person came forth. During his teens and twenties the Christ as a gangling boy became a handsome man. He learned physical skills and gained strength and stamina. The sedentary life-style is always a temptation to us, and it is always a threat to our pioneering physically in the example of Jesus.

Third, he grew in grace by the side of God.—The King James version expression "in favor with God" is totally inadequate here. To think of Jesus as growing in favor with God would infer that he was courting God to win him over. This is not the meaning. Rather, being graced or gifted, Jesus was growing and blending his will into the plan of the Father as the Father patiently aided and guided him by his presence.

Finally, he grew in grace by the side of man.—Christ was open and exposed his life to people. He respected and earned respect. He was affectionate. He formed relationships. He was maturing and learning to be a friend to all people. These areas represent all of the potential growing areas of life. Actually each area offers no options, for each complements the other. They are meant to harmonize together. The training of the body, the discipline of the mind, the cultivation of character, and the opening of the spirit all total the possible wholeness available to each of God's people.

The Growth Example

Be assured we are not studying a mere biography. The verb has described a unique being in his pioneering venture. This person, this different being, is our valued example for growth. We each are different. As we mature we can and will develop our personal uniqueness. This is expected by God. However, Christ remains the common model for each of us. Through our individual growth we never lose our commonness with Christ. This has been made possible through the saving Christ who wills to be the living example for our growth.

The versatility of Abraham Lincoln is a constant amazement to me. Elton Trueblood, a Quaker Christian, has captured the essence of Lincoln's spiritual life in a work entitled *Abraham Lincoln, Theologian of American Anguish*. In his study Trueblood noted, "One of the important features of Lincoln's theology is the fact that it was a development. The man had an amazing ability to grow."[1] The emancipation President never lost the spirit of personal pioneering.

Sea pioneers dared to cross uncharted waters to this continent. Bold people pioneered to push back frontiers. Daring revolutionaries forged a nation and government. Men and women have challenged air, space, sea, and arctic regions. All these ventures are expressions of the pioneering principle inherent in humanity. While many frontiers have been conquered, nevertheless, the new land of the personal life is ever stretching out before us.

Note

1. Elton Trueblood, *Abraham Lincoln, Theologian of American Anguish* (New York: Harper & Row, 1973), p. 7.

10
My Daily Bread
Must Be Gathered

Greatness!

Wipe off your smug smile of feigned humility! Everyone courts some recognition.

Besides, a certain character of greatness is OK, if legitimately sought.

Greatness!

The term is too often reserved.

Lincoln, Churchill, and Wilson all displayed diplomacy and were called great.

Bruce Jenner has possessed unique athletic versatility, and many label him great.

Jonas Salk is revered for his research in poliomyelitis.

Fan clubs for stars of stage, screen, radio, and television come and go with the rise and the fall of the great entertainers. We do not debate their greatness. They have public acclaim. They are recognized by the products of their talents and "the breaks." Their clubs are small, fragile, and always highly competitive.

Still, we outsiders, the nonalumni of the university of public recognition, continue to clamor for admittance into someone's scope of affirmation.

Good news!

A legitimate pursuit of personal *common greatness* is possible: *common greatness* that garners no headlines but may only be mentioned in the daily obituary column; *common greatness* that fosters no wealth but may be known only as a good credit risk; *common greatness* that does not include a list of earned degrees but may be recognized for having lived a disciplined life;

common greatness that is devoid of power or authority but may involve time spent carrying out other people's orders. Such possible, quiet, serene, day in and day out, personal magnitude is an accessible quest in the sometimes adjudged "ordinary" roles of life: the trusted spouse who is ready to listen and whose life is an open book to his mate; the wise parent busy being a good friend to his children and loving his spouse; the caring and concerned neighbor to whom you can be real; the concerned citizen who quietly exercises the right to vote and maintains his patriotic duty; the church member who responds when his church calls on him and sees his assigned role as worthy to the kingdom of God.

But how?

Such performances sound so blah, mundane, passive, indifferent, apathetic, dormant, even dilatory.

Besides, the 1980s are jubilant and exciting. I have aggressive energy ready to explode. I have abundant time that can't be wasted. I have urgent desires demanding satisfaction.

All such sound and fury today resembles cut flowers that soon wither and die. Clamoring for attention is like continuously eating junk food. You are filled but not nourished. Yesterday's headlines are just that—yesterday's headlines. The world of the last quarter of the twentieth century keeps demanding new and innovative exploits to keep the headlines. Usually champions and winning teams are soon forgotten. All in all, most broadcasting of greatness is deceptive in lasting effect and memory. Even Barnum and Bailey must keep adding new acts to keep drawing the same crowd year after year. The individual obsessed with a need for either constant peer recognition or national applause must keep outdoing his earlier feats. Most of us would soon burn out.

There *must* be some other way. There is! The quest for common greatness is satisfied in being a servant willing to gather daily bread from God.

Jesus was quite direct about greatness. In speaking to a large outdoor gathering, including his disciples, he said, "the greatest among you shall be your servant" (Matt. 23:11). He did not condemn greatness. Instead, he declared that the only acceptable and legitimate greatness is through servanthood.

Be frank, candid, honest, and sincere. Servanthood is offensive. The servant image waves the red flag of slavery before our eyes. The picture of the cruel and manipulative overseer demanding backbreaking labor by black slaves is repulsive to liberty lovers. We still are close enough to the days of American servitude to harbor the inescapable mental picture of a life-style of poverty, regimentation, and constant vulnerability to the beckoning call of the taskmaster.

Is Jesus' expectation irrelevant? Do we disregard or repudiate these words spoken prior to the era of American slavery? No! Common and ordinary greatness according to Jesus demands that we consider a certain characteristic of slavery.

A slave was a dependent person. Israel's life-style in Egypt was designed for dependence. The workday was structured. The sustenance was provided. The activity was limited. What the slave had, who the slave was, what the slave did, and why the slave did what the slave did were determined by the authority over him. We would be entirely wrong to think that the children of Israel walked out of Egypt and forgot the ravages of slavery. Vivid memories and remnants of a life-style remained. When they were first threatened by the armies of Egypt they responded in anger and emotional readiness to return in order to preserve their lives. At least an ordered life-style of dependence offered more safety. The Chosen People had not abandoned their dependent nature. Listen to the Exodus narration:

> And the whole congregation of the sons of Israel grumbled against Moses and Aaron in the wilderness. And the sons of Israel said to them, "Would that we had died by the Lord's hand in the land of Egypt, when we sat by the pots of meat, when we ate bread to the full; for you have brought us out into this wilderness to kill this whole assembly with hunger" (16:2-3).

Now God acted to use their dependency for his purpose.

Israel's trials and Egyptian bondage had been long, difficult, and cruel. Each individual had lived under the constant threat of death. God would not forget such sacrifice. He did not write off their years of sacrifice with a sigh of relief. He chose to redeem such pain and sorrow. While we do not charge the Egyptian enslavement to God's insistent will, he who allows calamity can also choose to use tragedy for his ongoing purpose. They had depended upon the taskmasters of Egypt out of fear. Now God was affirming their potential and ability to be dependent. He promised daily sustenance to them and called the nation to lean on him.

Remember these people were traveling. Their worries were legion. Keep contact with family members! Herd the stock! Be careful to avoid causing accidents! Don't lose the meager belongings! But God relieved them from the need to fret over food. In the wilderness there was no readily available food source. To kill one of their animals for food would mean destroying a means for living later when they were settled. So God promised a daily diet. He was appealing to a basic and undeniable need. He was saying, depend on me to feed you.

But God had a stipulation. "Gather of it [manna] every man as much as he should eat; you shall take an omer apiece according to the number of persons each of you has in his tent" (Ex. 16:16). Thus each man was instructed to gather and use only what he needed. But some tried the patience of God and Moses. They soon learned that God's provision could not be stored up. Leftover manna always spoils. Each man had to learn by experience that he must gather his daily bread each day. The servant who will be great will gather daily bread.

Bread? What is this bread? A multitude in Jesus' time pondered this same question.

> Our fathers ate the manna in the wilderness; as it is written, "He gave them bread out of heaven to eat." Jesus therefore said to them, "Truly,

truly, I say to you, it is not Moses who has given you the bread out of heaven, but it is My Father who gives you the true bread out of heaven. For the bread of God is that which comes down out of heaven, and gives life to the world." They said therefore to Him, "Lord, evermore give us this bread." Jesus said to them, "I am the bread of life; he who comes to Me shall not hunger" (John 6:31-35).

The daily bread is receiving day by day the presence of the living Christ into your life.

But I must come each day to gather the bread. Two people can be in the same room. But only until they acknowledge each other and begin to talk do they receive each other's presence. We live in God's world, but only in a day-by-day conversation in prayer and Scripture study do we know his presence. We have to come to him each day.

Too often we attempt to continue living on the sustenance of stale stuff. We run the risk of living off bread that was received a long time ago.

Occasionally, we are not very careful about what bread we gather into our life. Not all that even goes under the guise of gospel truth is nourishing food.

But how does this produce the common greatness? Such personal, satisfying magnitude comes through the *effect* of the daily bread received into your life.

When I Gather Daily Bread, I Keep a Day-by-Day Approach to Life

Examine your lifetime.

We naturally measure our time, at least, in terms of decades. When I turned forty a well-meaning friend kidded me, "At least the Bible promises you thirty more years."

A person living in the daily defiance of an incurable illness is comforted by his physician's promise of "a few good years." To be faced with the prognosis that you have a few months to live is indeed frightening and can be devastating.

My wife and I have been blessed with excellent health. However, in 1972 Lynn entered the hospital for corrective and preventive surgery. Actually the time chosen was more out of convenience than necessity. The doctor had indicated that, in time, the problem could impair her health but not immediately. Still the deficiency should eventually be corrected. She exercised the choice to proceed with surgery and prevent any future possible complications.

The afternoon before the operation the physician again assured us there was no reason to worry about complications, and, in fact, her recovery would be hastened by her excellent health.

The following morning Lynn went to surgery, and I waited in her room. We both possessed normal anxiety about the situation. In less time than I expected the doctor returned to her room. He, as kindly and compassionately as possible, proceeded to tell me there were complications. He had discovered an advanced malignancy.

The next day with his assistance I told her the whole truth. That evening no one came to the hospital to visit us. At first we felt alone. We were serving a church blessed, I thought, with a wholesome and genuine caring spirit. The people continually graced us with love. Throughout her illness numerous gestures of kindness were a source of consistent strength. But that June evening the absence of friends proved to be an occasion for a life-changing blessing. That evening in room 323 of Hinds General Hospital in Jackson, Mississippi, we faced her cancer directly and resolved for the rest of our lives to live one day at a time. During the next few days we began to experience liberation from the tyranny of time. Now waking together in the morning we receive the gift of another day in God's presence. Going to sleep each evening we entrust our care into the Lord's hands and hope for the coming day. Throughout each day, together or apart, we build moment altars and thank God for allowing us the blessing of one day at a time. True, sometimes we forget and become caught up in the expectation of future events and lose the glory of the present day. Then, conditioned by that experience over ten years ago and the gentle nudging of the God who is always there, we come back to bless the present day, a day that was so different from the day before and a day that will be assuredly different from the next.

Each day we all select tools to enable us to accomplish our prescribed tasks. These include pen and pencil, automobile, typewriter, hammer and nails, slide rule, textbook. Do we also include daily bread?

When I Gather Daily Bread, I Have Continuous Exposure to God

God created manna to satisfy Israel's food needs. More importantly though, the daily provision was intended to remind the people that God was still with them. The routine of gathering "morning by morning" (Ex. 16:21) was their daily opportunity to be reminded they were traveling in his presence.

We subscribe to the doctrine of the omniscience of God or the omnipresence of God. Most church members can quote Jesus' final promise "Lo, I am with you always" (Matt. 28:20). However, our daily actions frequently testify to an apathy concerning God's presence. We are prone to take God's unlimited presence in time and place for granted. The practice of gathering daily bread is an intentional effort to be redeemed from apathy and celebrate God's abiding presence.

Coming into his presence through gleaning daily bread:

We form a growing trust in the living God;

We refine our understanding that we are human and mortal and he is divine and eternal;

We become vulnerable to his will;

We cooperate in creating the possibility for him to surprise us.

When I Gather Daily Bread, I Admit I Cannot Handle Life Alone

Life in the 1980s is affected by a flood of fantasy and myth. The hero models for children include Wonder Woman, Bionic Man, the Incredible Hulk, E.T., and even Pac Man. Are we not hearing the clarion cries for power and authority that are beyond human capacity together with the dissatisfaction with mortal limitations? This is hypocrisy. Human beings were never meant to be self-sufficient and possess unlimited ability. Still the unrest with physical, emotional, and intellectual restrictions prevails.

Dave watched and waited upon his dying wife with patient and loving care. He confessed to me his greatest frustration. "I fought in World War II and Korea. I've always been strong. I've had jeeps blown out from under me and seen men blown to pieces, but this gets me. I cannot keep her from dying. I am not strong anymore." Surprising? The stress of human inability to accept weakness is a vicious self-imposed pressure. No one is totally sufficient and adequate for all seasons. But giving in to weakness, admitting limitations, and recognizing human boundaries are difficult tasks. Gathering daily bread brings us into the presence of the all-sufficient and all-powerful Father. He takes our weaknesses and blesses us with his strength. Daily exposure enables us to accept our humanity and be comfortable with being his creation.

When I Gather Daily Bread, I Will Change

Most of us harbor the common dislike for static. While buzz and crackle interrupt radio and television programs, static is even more offensive because it always remains the same. We readily expect changes in TV programming. We expect improvement in community life. Why do we not expect and accept change in self? Self-change is a threat. Self-change questions us. But self-change can be challenging and fulfilling.

Israel had become dependent in days of slavery. Bondage had made the Hebrews' life-style contingent on the whims of the selfish authorities. Then God liberated them. They left a livelihood of dependence based on fear. Then God offered to provide for the freed people. The compassionate and caring Father offered his grace to the people in daily food. In such grace he made possible to them the opportunity to know him as both liberator and provider. They believed that he liberated them. Now he revealed himself as provider. Coming day by day to gather his food they could receive him as the God who daily provided for their needs. The people changed by an expanded concept of God.

You and I cannot be in daily contact with God and remain the same. In his presence we discover more of his nature; we acknowledge more of his claims on us; we recognize more of his purpose for us. We cannot stay as we are.

Mister Tom was a robust and vigorous man. Past seventy years of age, he lived alone and pursued the patient work of a stonemason. Carlyle Marney tells of his attraction to the man and his discovery of Mr. Tom's higher type of devotion.

> I happened by his trailer in mid-afternoon. He had stopped late for lunch, had first taken a nap. When he awakened he had broiled a piece of meat out of his own locker and with a great chunk of bread was enjoying his lunch when I dropped in for a visit. I noticed a book open on the table and casually, perhaps too curiously, glanced over his shoulder; he was reading the New Testament. Apparently it was a habit of his to build himself little altars through the day; not out of rock, not out of mortar, but out of high thoughts he reads.[1]

The common life is made great through gathering daily bread.

Note

1. Carlyle Marney, *Beggars in Velvet* (New York: Abingdon Press, 1960), p. 14.

11
My Life Is Best Faced with Faith

Several years ago the eminent Scottish New Testament scholar, William Barclay, wrote his *Spiritual Autobiography*. One chapter is entitled "I Believe." In the opening statement he affirms, "Sooner or later this chapter has to be written."[1] Such a chapter in each person's life is inescapable.

We are *faithers*.

Inevitably we will faith something. We possess a need to faith that longs for satisfaction. We trust our neighbors to respect our property and goods. We depend upon the validity of government regulations to safeguard our food and protect our health. We expect schools to present creditable truth to our children. We make daily purchases with the belief that a product is as it was advertised.

However, faith in God is an entirely different dimension. The Christian religion rests on faithing that God is as he is revealed in Jesus Christ. Is there any part of the gospel more basic than the belief that God is? How do we know Jesus Christ revealed the nature of God? Yes, the Scriptures present the incarnate Son of God. But wherein rests the credibility of Scripture? The entire foundation and superstructure for the essence of Christianity is our faith in God. The truth of Christianity is only validated by our faith in God.

Declare your security in salvation by grace, in the knowledge that once saved, you are always saved. We receive this affirmation of our worth through faith in God. How do we enjoy the peace that life is extended beyond the grave? We faith the God of all eternity.

In addition, faith in God is the Christian's means of handling life. Faith in God will not solve all the problems and may not even affect some. But faith will make us able to see a situation through. Paul in Colossians merely mentioned a fellow disciple named Demas. Later, as he wrote to Timothy, he said, "Demas having loved this present world, has deserted me" (2 Tim. 4:10). Apparently, Demas did not faith God to see his ministry through.

Personal faith in the living God enables:

The businessman facing Monday morning to welcome the week of calls, paperwork, interruptions and increasing stress;

The sleepless invalid to lose the loneliness of the hours ahead as she awaits the dawn of another day;

The teacher walking into the classroom to offer words that will be heard and understood while being tempted to be impatient;

The engineer facing the problem that was not supposed to happen to emerge from the maze;

The family member who seems to have lost touch with his spouse or sibling to take the initiative to restore the ties;

The church member whose tongue has caused hurt, isolation, guilt, and hostility to have the courage to say, "Please forgive me";

The housewife who is constantly faced with the task of administering a social unit called family, to receive daily wisdom as referee, cook, maintenance supervisor, and bookkeeper;

You and me in all of life to possess the patience and the knowledge that we are not alone.

But how do *you* define your faith in God? Recently I sat down at my desk with a pencil and piece of paper to reflect upon the question, What is faith in God to me? I intensely desired to deal with the challenge myself, alone. I had to push away Tillich's "Faith as Ultimate Concern," Luther's obsession with *"Sole Fide,"* Bonhoeffer's "Faith Out of Obedience," and even Isaiah's "Strength not to faint." I discovered in that sobering escape from theological culture that I had to begin by analyzing my past experiences of faith in God.

Faith in God was the anticipated joy engulfing me on both

occasions I signed papers to adopt children.

Faith in God was trustful waiting as the decision was made to stay with a specific doctor during a health crisis when around me well-meaning friends offered advice concerning different physicians and different hospitals.

Faith in God was agony as together with the church family we searched for answers to pressing issues upon which God's people had to take a stand.

Faith in God was the choice to refuse a denominational position out of the conviction my work was not completed in a pastorate.

Looking back I can label those experiences as faith times. In retrospect I know when I faithed. Living in the present I draw from this treasury of faith times, for each past experience conditions each other faith adventure into the future. But my experience is not meant to be normative for you. I can only share what faith in God is to me. Still, how do I know my faith in God is legitimate? I compare my faith experience with that of a Bible character whose life demonstrated human and honest faith in God. I refer to Abraham, that Old Testament patriarch who was awarded his place in history because of his faith in God. A review of the major events of his life is a study in the pilgrimage of faith.

Faith in God Is an Adventure

Abraham, the son of Terah, is a patriarch claimed by Jews, Muhammadans, and Christians alike; but the real importance of the man rests in the fact that he trusted God to guide him. Initially, he qualified as the faithful one for responding to God's call to go out, "not knowing where he was going" (Heb. 11:8).

Abraham was a man of adventure. What a synonym for life!

Adventure! Various views of living share degrees of attraction. Some folks endure but curse their days. Others exist by the theme "What will be, will be." Only the people of faith in God are keenly aware of life as adventure with God. They know faith as a verb.

Have you ever wondered why the classic tales of *Swiss Family Robinson, Robinson Crusoe,* and *Gulliver's Travels* never go out of style? Who can grow tired of the stories of Daniel Boone and the exploits of Lewis and Clark? What child abandons a Bobbsey Twins, Nancy Drew, or Hardy Boys story half read? All are accounts of adventure, stories told by verbs. Regularly they are our substitutes for the adventures we never took. Would it not be a tragedy if we missed the adventure of living life with faith in God? Herein is a most attractive and winsome reason for salvation through faith in Christ.

The adventure of faith in God is moving always toward the future. The move is toward the great yet-to-be which will be, and we will be a part of it. In faithing God we can help God's future happen. Yes, future in the potential sense belongs to God, and he invites us in to harmonize our future with him to make his future happen. This can be done only through faith.

The great result, though, will be change. Abraham left Ur. The metropolis was quite advanced as a trade and commercial center and excelled in art, medicine, and law. Abraham's family enjoyed a happy and secure life. Ur was home to them. God called the patriarch to leave home. Such a call always means change. Ignorant of God's intended destination Abraham was open and exposed to changes he could not envision.

Faith in God always guarantees coming changes. Initial faith in God accompanied by grace brings salvation and demands immediate change as a person experiences the beginning of a new life. And God keeps on changing us. Personal growth is synonymous to life in God's kingdom. Growth never happens apart from change.

Abraham did eventually reach the Promised Land, but he never possessed it. His ultimate task was to wander, explore, and wait. In the midst of change, sometimes patience is the prevailing demand. Sometimes we never see the end of the adventure but have to serve as the agents of change and bequeath the joys of change to later generations.

A man named Robert Mills won the 1835 competition to design a fitting monument to George Washington. Yet inadequate funds, apathy, and politics prevented the structure's completion until 1884. Mills did not live to see the completed monument and know public acclaim for his work.

Leonardo Da Vinci was far beyond his times. Today we recognize his paddleboat as Robert Fulton's accomplishment. His horseless carriage dream was Henry Ford's Model A. His hope for a flying machine was realized by the Wright brothers. A magnificent part of faith in God is envisioning changes that you hope to make even though you may not live to see them.

Faith in God Requires Living

Trite?

I find the expression "By faith he lived" (Heb. 11:9) most intriguing. Abraham lived as a nomad looking for a city. Don't rush to ask what kind of city. Consider first his nomadic life-style. Genesis clues us in to his life pattern.

Abraham faithed God as he knelt at Shechem to begin the rhythm of his life—building altars then rising to move on (Gen. 12:7).

Abraham listened to the news of famine and faithed God as he adjusted his intended journey to go for a season into Egypt. His doing so reminds us that along the way circumstances may interrupt our planned journeys (Gen. 12:10).

Abraham was very human as he plotted with Sarah and succumbed to manipulation and lying to Abimelech. Even in the midst of faith in God we can make mistakes (Gen. 20:1-18).

Abraham faithed God as he entered the role of diplomat to offer the first choice of land to Lot and graciously take the second-best land. To faith God may require us to play second fiddle (Gen. 12:5-13).

Abraham faithed God as he interceded for ten righteous men in Sodom and took the initiative to save Lot from Sodom and its terror. Faith in God often requires bold action (Gen. 18:22-33).

Each incident was part of the life of a man living with only the earthly security of his tent pegs in the ground. Still he looked for a city, a new home, a new heaven, and the fulfillment of God's promise. But even in looking he never ceased to be busy living.

Faith in God Brings Surprises

Abraham became a father at the age of one hundred years. What a startling surprise through faith in God! Yes, the child had been promised, and Abraham believed the promise. Still, we reckon the birth of Isaac as a faith surprise. When you faith God, be prepared, for God may break in with his extra, his plus, his smile of a special blessing along the way.

History's greatest faith journey was the Exodus. As Moses led God's people out of Egypt, great surprises came out of their often weak faith. God spoke from a mountain, gave laws, and taught his people how to govern themselves. Jehovah gave instructions for a tabernacle and a system of worship which became the center of their life in society. God set his daily table with manna and quail and met their hunger. When we take the trip of faith in God we must be ready for the surprises.

According to an old Persian fairy tale, a wise king named Fafer, the monarch of Serendip, had three handsome sons, each possessing great potential. The king, desiring the best education for his sons, sent them to travel throughout the world. Their travels brought great and unexpected treasures to each of them. The tale provided the occasion to coin the term *serendipity*—to describe the unexpected discoveries or treasures of life. Along the way the person of faith in God will experience God's great serendipities:

Good news following serious surgery or strength to face threatening life emergencies;

A child's high fever breaking in the middle of the night;

Insight into a Scripture passage never seen before;

The means to weather a financial emergency;

Recognition of a job well done when you thought you did your worst;

Meeting that special person you hoped to one day encounter to whom you can open your life and discover a whole new dimension of friendship.

Faith in God is always serendipitous. That's the way faith in God is. When we trust God along the way, he adds other great and unexpected joys to our life.

Faith in God Means Testing

Picture Abraham, Isaac, and the small donkey loaded with wood making their way to Mount Moriah. This is a most difficult passage to understand, especially for parents. We can only begin to imagine Abraham's solemn thoughts. He was facing the supreme test. He was struggling to be willing to offer up his son in sacrifice.

The only way I can understand the scenario is to recognize the event as a preview of the coming Savior and his sacrifice. This event must be set within the total biblical context. When God stopped Abraham he was saying to us, "I would not require the ultimate sacrifice of you, Abraham. I cannot make you go through with Isaac's death; I can only require this of me and my willing Son." This is as far as Abraham's test would go.

The person of faith will be tried. God is neither sadistic nor playing games, but in trials we discover our own depth of faith in God and we learn to mature. A test is always an opportunity for faith in God to grow us.

In April 1966 I sat with ten fellow students to take the qualifying examinations for admission to the graduate school of New Orleans Baptist Theological Seminary. Our first exam was an essay test. We were to be given the subject, a pencil, paper, and two hours. All of us had attempted to guess the exam subject. The death of God controversy was the major theological issue at that time. We each had read articles on Christian atheism and felt we were adequately prepared. The professor gave each of us a small strip of paper folded up almost like a spitball. He told us to read the subject and begin writing.

I opened the piece of paper and quickly read the topic. The death of God controversy was in no way involved in the assigned task. The instructions read, "You have two hours to compose an essay on the subject, 'Contemporary Problems in Biblical Hermeneutics.'" I immediately felt green and sick with a high flavoring of doubt, anger, and loneliness. It seemed that I was totally by myself. Gradually the icy moments of solitary existence began giving away, and I began to experience a strange companionship. There was no revelation of hermeneutical definitions or content for the essay. Rather, the words came, "Don't give up." I began to think, and soon I began to write. Within this faith experience I began to realize I was not totally alone. In that episode of agonizing trauma I found a new realness of faithing the living God.

Note

1. William Barclay, *A Spiritual Autobiography* (Grand Rapids: Eerdmans, 1975), p. 34.

12
I Am a Professional Amateur Christian

We plague children with the question "What do you want to be when you grow up?" Their quick and ready answers might include firefighter, nurse, policeman, teacher, astronaut, missionary, or athlete. Recently a father in our town announced with dismay his son's fascination with the city garbage truck. "My son is obsessed with the desire to be a garbage man." That's quite OK. After all, the boy has chosen work that is honorable and often taken for granted.

However, the combination of the question "What do you want to be" and the child's usual response in terms of describing a job is indeed a parable of confusion. We ask, "What do you want to be?" and the answer is given in terms of doing. We adults accept such a response as if being and doing were the same. Tragically, this question and answer process is a symptom of our failure to acknowledge the difference in what we do and who we are.

Man has always been threatened by the confusion and amalgamation between who he is and what he does. Take for instance, the biblical scenario of Cain and Abel. Each brought an offering, products of their work. Apparently Cain did not give God his best. God's response was his recognition that Cain's act of worship in offering his gift did not show proper reverence and respect. The *Good News Bible* aids us here. Cain, "If you had done the right thing, you would be smiling; but because you have done evil, sin is crouching at your door. It wants to rule you, but you must overcome it" (Genesis 4:7). God's displeasure was a response to Cain's action. However, Cain allowed God's justice to affect his personality. He became angry. Literally, it became hot for him. Rage and hostility were allowed to grow until the elder son murdered his brother. Cain could not accept God's displeasure for his action and at the same time know that God still cared for him. The confusion between action and being resulted in disaster.

Our society has birthed great confusion between being and having. Legions of marketplaces and city malls plus stores along rural roads abound with gadgets advertised as quick solutions to household chores. Ready credit is usually available. We may not use the tool we purchase once a year, but we have it. Besides, in time, the periodic yard or garden sale will enable a neighbor to have it. Our American economic system demands that advertisers keep telling us how much we need their products. Usually we act on their suggestions. Such purchases are but surface symbols of a deeper fallacy. We have learned too well that we must develop our power to have. Subsequently we are caught. We must have. Then when face to face with self all we can see is what we have.

Imagine yourself with nothing. Is this possible? Are you afraid? Really, for a moment just try to strip yourself of everything and come to grips with whether or not you have value apart from what you have or do. Can you persevere? Or do you fear emotional paralysis, shame, or even death if you were cut off from all the trappings and gadgets that you possess or the work that you do? We come into this world naked and we go out helpless, but between the cradle and the grave we spend most of our time clutching or reaching for something or trying to stay busy. Unless we are rescued and receive him who said, "I come to set the captives free," we will live a life of much disaster.

Confusion between what we have and who we are and the dilemma of distinction between who we are and what we do have invaded the spiritual realm. These confusions are enemies of the Christian faith. Let me illustrate. Are you a Christian? What answers come to your mind? Usually we answer the question concerning our Christianity based on the religious things we do. We go to church. We give. We teach a Sunday School class. We serve on a committee. And while it is true that Christianity is a religion of action, the faith that moves us to act and live a moral life with an aggressive witness to the living Christ must be an expression of who we are as individual Christians. If not, we are false, hypocritical. We lie. Only if our nature is right will what we do really be effective.

When we visit the doctor for a physical examination, he, in a sense, is looking over our physical being to determine how well we can function. I wonder how much attention we give to our spiritual maintenance.

Concern for the body often outweighs concern for individual Christian being. However, it is never too late to give attention to God's expected nature for us. This is not to say that we are to be carbon copies of one another. We are not intended to be spiritual clones. May I suggest a comprehensive term that is adequate to describe the nature that we must possess as Christians—the Christian, a professional amateur.

Christian

What is a Christian?

Do we define a Christian by what he is not? He is not a Jew, Muslim, Hindu, Buddist, agnostic, or atheist.

Do we define the Christian by what he does? He attends, he gives, he serves.

Let's travel back before the day of the first Christian and see if there is a definition that is more conclusive.

According to Matthew, Jesus began his public ministry and almost immediately extended a call to some people to join with him. He said to those fishermen, "Follow Me, and I will make you fishers of men" (Matt. 4:19). Carefully analyze the two parts of his summons. Jesus was saying first, "I want a relationship with you." This invitation is emphasized even more as you notice in John 1 that as Jesus was talking with Philip and Nathaniel and some unnamed disciples he invited the group to come along with him. This was his request for them to spend some time with him.

Several years ago I met a man whom I had always held in high regard. He was a pastor model to me. After we visited awhile he said to me, "I want to get to know you better." I reflect on that statement as one of the most affirming things that has ever happened in my life. He was saying, "I would like to have a relationship with you." This was Jesus' intention in speaking to the disciples. When we are born we are cut loose. We are alone. But we need a presence with us that knows no barriers. We need a presence that is never cut off in any way and is always the same. This is what Christ offers to us.

Jesus, secondly, promised a change to those who would have a relationship with him. The term speaks of a creative act of change. He was saying, "I will continue making you to become." Jesus was forecasting the creative work he would bring forth in their lives.

Jesus' desire to have a relationship with these men and bring change to their lives was fundamental evangelism. When Christ forms a relationship with us and promises and gives change he creates the Christian person. Upon this definition we can build a foundation for understanding what it is to be a professional, amateur Christian.

Professional

We live and die, come and go, in a world of professionals— engineers, teachers, doctors, lawyers, accountants, and vocational Christian workers. We like professional identity. But what qualifies you as a professional? You might answer: my education, my skill, or my success. These are the usual answers we give. There is a criteria more basic to being a professional than those we have listed. You see, somebody at some time awarded you the credentials that made you a professional. This may have come through your proficiency, from some recognized authority, or from practical experience. But a professional is always awarded the credentials to be a professional. Sometimes an official license of recognition is awarded by some governing agency. The authority may be as basic as a diploma from high school. I remember very vividly an old black pastor in our town. He used to ask me to type his sermons. One year he was scheduled to deliver the baccalaureate address at our high school. I shall never forget the first statement of his sermon. He said, "You have finished that you may begin." He was recognizing the graduates by awarding verbal credentials for completing their preparation for the future.

Sometimes our credentials are unofficial recognitions. Abraham Lincoln had no degrees, but when he was elected President of the United States he was awarded the credentials of a professional. Many years ago a small community in East Tennessee had a very fine doctor. In the later years of his life the doctor took a young man under his tutelage and tried to teach him everything he knew about medicine. The old country doctor died, and the community was left without a physician. The people of the community petitioned the Tennessee legislature to grant this young man a license to practice medicine in their town. Only once in the history of Tennessee has the legislature granted a license to practice to someone who had not been to medical school. They were giving the young man the recognition and awarding him credentials. I have many beautiful memories of farmers sitting in my father's blacksmith shop on Saturday afternoons talking about the crops and weather. Invariably they would discuss different farmers in their area and describe their fields, planting procedures, and cultivating methods. I was interested to hear them talk of those they recognized as good and productive farmers. They were awarding them credentials. But what credentials qualify us to be professional Christians? They, like all credentials, are given.

Matthew 16 records a meeting between Jesus and his disciples. The Master began with a question addressed to the entire group. "Who do people say that the Son of Man is?" (v. 13). Already he had indicated that he was Lord of the sabbath, that he had the authority to forgive sin, and that God was his Father. But he wanted to know if he was known for his true being. He was asking them to tell him if people were recognizing his true nature. You see, God keeps coming through just as he is; but the question continues, Do we see him as he is? Jesus was saying, "I want to know if you are seeing me just as I am." Their answers were quite surprising. "Some say John the Baptist; and others, Elijah, but still others, Jeremiah, or one of the prophets" (v. 14). They were indicating, "Lord, people are still struggling for your true identity." This was no problem to Jesus. The difficulty lay with those who were looking toward him. People today still struggle to understand the real identity of Jesus Christ.

Jesus then moved in more specifically. "Who do you say that I am?" (v. 15). This question was directed with the great emphasis to all the disciples. He was trying to help them decide which group they thought was right. There must have been a period of silence. Then Simon said, "You are the Christ, the Son of the living God" (v. 16, RSV). Eureka! Peter expressed his personal discovery and exercised his responsibility to confess and profess Christ.

Once we claim and profess the true nature of Jesus Christ he then gives us our identity. He then clears before our eyes who we are after we profess who he is.

Have you ever walked through a house of mirrors? Some mirrors make you taller than you are. Some mirrors show you broader than you are. Some of the mirrors even reveal your body parts in ill proportion. You see, these mirrors are designed for distortion. They do their job well. Go outside the house of mirrors and stand before a normal mirror, and you see yourself just as you really are. Our Christ is the normal mirror against whom we can really see who we are once we profess who he really is. For Peter that day was a time to become a professional. Because he claimed and professed Christ just as he really was, Peter received his credentials. Jesus said, "You are Peter" (v. 18).

This was affirmation for Peter's courage, boldness, and willingness to risk himself. Here Peter received his credentials from God. The credentials by which we become a professional Christian are always given to us by the grace of God.

Notice that Jesus reminded Peter that his profession was not a human conclusion or personal assessment alone. The profession came from heaven. Such is the only way that Christ can be known. Jesus Christ must be experienced. God recognizes our profession of who he is and responds by rewarding us the credentials. These credentials come through a discovery, and that is another name for faith.

My children have given me the credential—Dad. My wife awards me the credential—husband. Church members have extended the credential—pastor. My acquaintances grace me with the credential—friend. But it is God through Jesus Christ who gives me the credentials of a Christian. They are always given. I do nothing to earn them. So the Christian is a professional and also an amateur.

Amateur

Confused? Probably you think this is a contradiction. How can I be both professional and amateur? Well, the only realm in which the roles are possibly synonymous is the Christian faith.

A few days before Christmas several years ago a major television network aired a program entitled "A Christmas Without Snow." This most interesting drama depicted a community church in a large metropolitan area. The volunteer choir was rehearsing to present Handel's *Messiah*.

The church had employed a choir director for the single performance. His disposition was rigid, authoritarian, and perfectionistic. The musicians had labored through several rehearsals. Remember, this choir was made up entirely of volunteers. The night arrived for the solo parts to be assigned, and the credentials were to be awarded for the solo parts. The choir included one member who had earlier received professional voice training. She assumed that she would be awarded the solo lead without any question. However, as the choir director made the solo announcements she was not included. In true bucolic language she "missed the spout when the glory came out." At that point in the drama the camera focused in on the frustrated lady. Her growing rage and hostility were evident. She was infuriated. Finally she leaped to her feet and unleashed her pent-up anger. She was humiliated for having been overlooked, especially because of her professional ability. She declared her disgust and feeling of superiority to the other members of the choir.

She lashed out, "You are just a bunch of amateurs." Then she stormed out of the room. A quietness, one of those agonizing moments of existential hurt, settled in over the rest of the members of the choir. Then, after a short period of silence the choir director slowly responded, "You realize she is absolutely right. You are a gathering of amateurs." What was happening here? Was he sprinkling salt in the new wound? Then the choir director continued with a bit of smile, "Yes, you are amateurs in the best original and generic sense of that word." He said, *"Amor* is the Latin origin of that word. I remind you that *amor* means to love, and amateurs are those who do something because they love it." We must see ourselves as *professional amateur* Christians. That which is called Christian must be done because we love it.

Now let's go back to the New Testament. Our scene is one of the final events in Jesus' earthly ministry. The resurrected Christ appeared on the shore of the Sea of Tiberias and invited his disciples to come to breakfast with him. They had been fishing all night and had no fish. A voice from the shore cried out, "Cast the nets on the righthand side of the boat, and you will find a catch" (John 21:6). Their obedience brought forth a gigantic catch. In the midst of the astonishment John said to Peter, "It is the Lord" (John 21:7). Peter leaped out of the boat and swam ashore while the others tugged at the nets and made their way to the seashore. There Jesus had already prepared breakfast. He extended them an invitation to break their fast with him. Quietness prevailed. This was no time for questions. The occasion was holy. The Bible says, "None of the disciples ventured to question Him, 'Who are You?' knowing that it was the Lord" (John 21:12). Doubt was absent. Understanding was present.

Soon after breakfast Jesus initiated a conversation with Simon Peter. Jesus called him Simon, an expression of intimacy but pregnant with the reminder to Simon of his old life. Probably Jesus wanted Simon to remember the inconsistencies in his life. Jesus posed a question for his impulsive friend. "Simon, . . . do you love Me more than these?" (John 21:15). The question was really, Simon, are you ready now to become an amateur? Simon, you have professed me. You have received the credentials that I awarded you. Now you have to face the question concerning whether or not you are ready for amateur status.

What a reversed process from our Western culture! We usually elevate the amateur to the professional. The golfer who reaches a recognized degree of proficiency as an amateur announces one day that he is going to turn pro. In the Christian faith, though, we move from professional up to amateur. We garner the credentials from God that enable us to be a pro. Then we have to face the choice concerning whether or not we can accept the call to be an amateur and accept amateur status.

Jesus and Peter had quite a discussion. The question "Do you love me?" kept coming back to Simon. The question was inescapable. Peter was faced now with his agonizing call to accept amateur status.

Did he become an amateur? You only have to look into the opening pages of the Book of Acts to see the man who was willing to do what he did because he loved Christ. Peter as depicted in Acts possessed a genuine sense of compulsion and aggressiveness as a Christian amateur.

What is your identity, your nature, your being as a Christian?

Are you a Christian follower? Do you claim to have a relationship with Christ and the desire for change? You may answer, "Sure, I want his presence. I need his relationship with me because I don't want to get lost in life."

Maybe you even consider yourself a pro. That sounds good. Have you acknowledged the reception of the credentials that have been awarded you through his grace?

Are you ready for amateur status? We claim our professional identity through grace, but amateur status is realized only as we answer the question "Are we being Christian and doing his will because we love him?"

13
My Weapons Are Adequate for My Struggle

Goliath!

The oversized brute in the Bible reminds me that I must fight my battles with my own weapons and armor.

What if David had attempted to face Goliath using Saul's armor and wielding the king's sword?

You remember the story.

David left his home in Bethlehem intending to deliver grain, cheese, and bread to his brothers in combat. Arriving in the valley of Elah, he was astonished by the fear and cloud of paralysis afflicting the mighty army of Israel. Goliath of Gath, one man, a giant of a man, daily defied and intimidated the soldiers. David's own brothers announced the frustration of the whole army by their hostile embarrassment upon his arrival. Never threatened by his kinsmen's shame, the baby boy of Jesse's house volunteered to fight the hero of the Philistines.

The rationale of putting a shepherd lad against the Gath giant was pushed aside as a desperate king championed the boy to "go, and may the Lord be with you" (1 Sam. 17:37). Quickly Saul's conditional faith and/or prevailing doubts surfaced as he insistently offered his personal armor and sword to David. Out of respect for the king the courageous youth modeled the armor, lifted the heavy sword, and attempted to walk. Alone, facing wild predators, the shepherd boy had learned to fight without the protection and unencumbering weight of heavy weapons. Thus he knew the king's well-meant offering would prove to be more of a liability than an asset. David fought Goliath armed only with his sling, his staff, and a few carefully selected stones. He was the victor. He had dared to stand before the superman, the colossal human, the seemingly invincible symbol of the Philistines. With his sling in hand he boldly cried, "This day the Lord will deliver you up into my hands . . . that all this assembly may know that the Lord does not deliver by sword or by spear; for the battle is the Lord's and He will give you into our hands" (1 Sam. 17:46-47).

Again, what if David had approached Goliath wearing Saul's coat of mail and helmet of brass, dragging the unwieldy sword? Such a question must be confined to the annals of everlasting mystery. The truth stands clear—God went into battle with a small boy who was willing to use his own weapons to fight his chosen giant. Might can be slain through faith in God. But even accompanied by God we are expected to battle with our own weapons. In addition to the weight and restrictiveness of Saul's battle apparel was the fact that David had never tested them. The confrontation with Goliath was too crucial for a trial run with untested fighting clothes and weapons.

Life is synonymous with struggle, conflict, contention, strain, collision, striving, discord, strife, and antagonism against giants of many descriptions, sizes, and strengths.

At 7:54 AM Eastern Daylight Time, May 20, 1927, Charles Lindbergh lifted the nose of the *Spirit of St. Louis* off the runway of Roosevelt Field on Long Island. Inside the tiny plane one man attempted to fly the vast Atlantic armed with a sextant, compass, and chart. He faced the vast expanse of water cognizant of the frailty of his airplane and the necessity of making seven course changes mostly over water. He defied distance, skeptics, and the fact that his attempted feat had never been completed before.[1] Lindbergh was not blind to his giant.

Richard E. Byrd elected to spend seven months alone in the immense frozen wasteland of the Antarctic.[2] The survival facility, a prefab shack, would not accommodate three men, the proven number and arrangement for such a discipline. Two men alone would prove to be psychological menaces to each other. Byrd alone set his face toward the persistent and increasing cold, heavy darkness, and over six months' isolation. Much of the time he struggled with the will to live as a leaky oil stove poisoned him with carbon monoxide fumes. Through the whole ordeal of nausea, headaches, debilitating weakness, and wonder about his own sanity he refused to acknowledge the growing giant to his friends 125 miles away. Byrd's original purpose in moving to the advance camp was to observe weather phenomena in the cold continent. That priority became secondary. In the midst of in-depth exposure to himself and reliance on years of discipline of mind and body he made the awesome discovery of the beauty of just being alive.

Sam Houston completed with applause his tenure as the first president of the Texas republic. The hero of San Jacinto was affirmed for his military savvy, statesmanship, and bold leadership. Mirabeau Bonaparte Lamar succeeded the bold adventurer, and all Houston had fought to build quickly deteriorated. In December 1841 The Raven again assumed the leadership of the republic, saddled by a currency worth three cents per American dollar, a treasury depleted below the ability to buy firewood for the president's residence, the threat of invasion by Santa Anna, and combined debts of at least seven million and possibly twelve million dollars, all owed in gold. In Houston's own words to the Texas congress, "It seems that we have arrived at a crisis."[3] Houston looked his giant straight in the eye.

Giants tramp our land today, giants that create in us the sobering question, Can I cope with . . .

Prolonged and extended illness accompanied by limited activity, erosion of physical stamina, deterioration of thinking and aggravated reliance on kinfolk or friends for daily care;

Vocation change requiring alteration of daily routine, reduction in salary, and abandonment of natural skills for training in a new task;

Unrealized dreams, for, inevitably, we all must settle for less in life than we expected;

Divorce and the residue of guilt and anger left to fester into grief—for the marriage break-up is, without exception, a loss, and everyone involved is left less than what they were before;

caring for aged parents—for with love and genuine appreciation for those who gave you life come the startling realizations that they move more slowly than their children, exist on a diet of bland food, and call each ache and pain another red flag signaling the final end;

Unexpected financial emergencies ranging from fitting the cost of a broken tooth into a lean, tight budget to the shock of realizing you have inadequate medical insurance and may have made deficient preparations for your children's college educations;

Disability and the anxious frustration effected by the incapacity to "do as you please" and the necessity of continually attempting to medicate a wounded ego;

Addiction—the total surprise that a family member is dependent on drugs or alcohol or an obsession with work or disgust with work that has created an obsession to satisfy a need for thrills;

Self-dislike—I've got *me* on my hands and what do I do?

And the list continues beyond any one person's imagination.

Help!

Often the origin of our advancing despair in the presence of giants rests either in our own failure to discover our God-given armor and weapons or the fact that we have sold out to using someone else's tools of war.

Other Folks' Weapons and Armor

Saul first offered David his personal battle attire, ornate and attractive garments, the symbol of regal authority. The war dress commanded respect for the wearer and was designed for comfort—to protect the king's body from his armor. This was Saul's robe, designed and sewn for him. For David to wear the sign of the king into battle would have been deceptive. David was unwilling to pawn himself off in hypocritical dress.

Saul trusted his armor to protect him. The wearing of armor always shields the wearer from full exposure to the enemy. While such defensive technique is necessary in battle, David opted to enter the arena without this protection.

Saul handed David his own sword, a weapon for defense and attack. How impractical for David! Consider the lad's size and reach compared to the giant's range with spear, javelin, and sword. The shepherd boy had no battle plan that included close range combat. Saul meant well in attempting to prepare David for battle, but the son of Jesse saw no advantage in wearing another man's armor and sword.

People, well-meaning friends, are often ready to supply us with their armor and sword. "I know what you are up against; let me tell you how I handled that dilemma." Careful, that friend is reflecting on his means of survival through his traumatic experience. There is strength in shared experiences, but each person has unique problems. No difficulty has an exact carbon copy. The same circumstances are never repeated.

News of my wife's cancer brought many suggestions from well-meaning friends offering names of doctors, addresses of hospitals, and convictions about miracle drugs plus advice in preparing for reactions to treatment. The flood of persuasive counsel had the potential to inundate us. We faced the need to map out a course, trust God, pray, rely on one medical procedure at a time, nurture each other emotionally, and receive life one day at a time. Having passed over that giant I often feel tempted and qualified to tell cancer patients how we coped. I must volunteer testimony to God's act to save her, but I have no right to impose our chosen approach to cancer upon anyone else. That would be robbery and a futile attempt to program God.

The Scripture pictures Saul hastily dressing David and putting the sword in his hand. Standing before the king all suited up, hand clutching the heavy sword, David must have asked, "Do I face Goliath as my king desires, or do I encounter the giant as I desire?" Such a movement of truth is inevitable. The pressure and offering of other folks' weapons and swords causes us to candidly question and compare our abilities. David refused the cumbersome war trappings of the king. Why? "I cannot go with these, for I have not tested them" (1 Sam. 17:39). His refusal was his choice to use weapons he could trust and rely on his own God-given ability.

My Weapons and Armor

When David shucked off the armor and handed back Saul's sword, he asserted his integrity and freedom. Putting down Saul's weapons he chose to be only David, no one else.

Picture the lad, ready, anxious to fight Goliath. He is not wearing Saul's coat. He refused to be mistaken as a king. He wears no man's armor; his defense mechanism far exceeded dependence on outward resistance. God was present in his life. He carried his stick, his own sling, and stones he had chosen. The Scriptures' tone is strong in expressing that these specific weapons belonged to him (1 Sam. 17:40). But another cache of arms also sustained the shepherd boy.

Physical strength and stamina, the yield of long hours of disciplined labor, enabled him to walk toward Goliath agile and alert. Previous encounters with vicious predators stalking his sheep had mustered courage. Each step toward the giant was accompanied by a sense of right. Still, his most powerful weapon was a firm dependence on the living God.

Only David, son of Jesse, ordained to be king of Israel, was intended to fight this original Goliath. His battle is now over. The story is preserved as a reminder that each man must use his own personal weapons to face his foes. My giants have names other than Goliath. I encounter them in locations other than the valley of Elah. My collision with my Titans may not capture headlines or rate as subject matter for an adventure story. My giants may not be big to you, but they are, nevertheless, my giants, my great tests; and you do not have the liberty to scoff and mock.

Saul must receive credit for allowing David to meet Goliath as he desired. David walked out confident in the potential of his sling and staff, and Saul graced him with room enough to prove his own weapons.

Besides, David was uniquely prepared. In the hills around Bethlehem the boy wonder had sharpened his skill with the sling but never anticipated that he would one day stand in front of the Israelite army and determine their destiny. Yet, in the moment of opportunity and responsibility, with the king's army behind him, he sized up the colossal human, recalled encounters before, banked on his known skills, and slew his giant with his weapons.

On February 11, 1861, President-elect Abraham Lincoln left Springfield, Illinois for Washington to assume the office of the presidency of a nation divided by slavery and the question of states' rights. The theoretical idea of a union of states was in jeopardy, and people North and South debated, argued, and skirmished over the powers and freedom of the several states. Abolitionists wanted a champion. Slaveholders feared any spokesman for freedom for all men. Minutes before the train pulled away from the station Lincoln walked out on the back platform of his car. He expressed appreciation and indebtedness to the crowd and the city of Springfield, and then he turned his attention to the future.

> I now leave, not knowing when or whether ever I may return, with the task before me greater than that which rested upon Washington. Without the assistance of that divine Being who ever attended him, I cannot succeed. With that assistance I cannot fail. Trusting in Him who can go with me, and remain with you, and be everywhere for good, let us confidently hope that all will yet be well.[4]

Lincoln met his giant. His weapons were adequate.

My next giant may be near. At first sight he may appear overpowering, invincible, and defiant. I must not allow him the satisfaction of making me panic. My weapons of grace, patience, kindness, forgiveness, flexibility, sensitivity, discomfort with wrong, readiness to accept change, and many others are adequate for my struggles.

Notes

1. Leonard Mosley, *Lindbergh* (New York: Dell Publishing Co., 1977), pp. 146-149.

2. Paul Rink, *Conquering Antarctica: Admiral Richard E. Byrd* (Chicago: Britannica Books, n.d.), p. 183.

3. Marquis James, *The Raven: A Biography of Sam Houston* (Atlanta: Mockingbird Books, 1929), pp. 263-264.

4. Carl Sandburg, *Abraham Lincoln: The Prairie Years,* I (New York: Dell Publishing Co. Inc., 1952), p. 320.

14
What Is God Really Doing in My Life?

Children's Letters to God is a delightful, amusing and thought-provoking little book. In one of the letters a child writes,

Dear God,
Could you write more stories? We have already read all the ones you have and begun again.[1]

Is God still writing stories now?

Carlyle Marney once endured what he termed a simultaneously exciting and difficult assignment. He was called on to present contemporary challenges to a group of Navy chaplains and to field their responses. Marney said he discovered in the long hours of dialogue that they wanted something more—they wanted God to say something![2]

What's God really up to? Even that question can be an escape if we assign only a theoretical, celestial, or ultimate significance to it.

Down here on earth in my own place, what is God doing in me? What is God doing in my life?

Honestly! Must I welcome the question? I cannot testify to God's spectacular or perennial activity in my life. I've known dry seasons and fruitful harvests, dormant spells and growing times, days of joy and times of sadness. Still my ambivalence is not excuse for rejecting the question.

Why do I even raise the question? Does some prevailing analytical need lurk inside me merely because some good teachers bequeathed to me an appreciation for legitimate questions?

Not altogether!

The question lies here before me and will not go away because the whole testament of my Christian faith is built on the premise that God got into me—to use Paul's term, "Christ in you" (Col. 1:27).

God, our God, was first introduced to most of us as a God of action, participation, and involvement. Genesis 1:1 reveals God creating. All successive verses of the Bible are the continued record of his doings in, with, and for his people. Throughout the long story, God was both zealous and jealous to link up his highest creation with himself, even those who often evaded his pursuit. The tie he desired was never satisfied by a passing acquaintance. The evidence of this holy quest is the whole life of Jesus Christ. Only reciprocal love conditioned by obedience was sufficient. The same God in Jesus Christ wooing past generations still seeks out his people. By grace I have become one sought and found.

He, God, is free to do solo work. Most of the time I do not acknowledge his activity. I live insensitive to his miraculous performance and too obsessed with my own goals. But he continually chooses to invite me, a subject of grace, into a cooperative venture with him. He will forgive my failure to affirm the changing season, falling rain, and even the natural bounty of the good earth. But he insistently seeks my awareness of his activity in my life.

Now following years of facing the question, often retreating but returning, the answer must be a personal one. What I know he is doing in me is known only in what I believe he is doing. I faith his activity in me.

You?

Only you with his help have the means to discover what he is doing in you. But I can offer suggestions out of the criteria of Scripture to guide both of us in discovering what God is up to in us.

In John 14 we find Jesus and a group of followers talking about the future. The entire chapter is saturated with the assurance that they would not be left alone. The Lord's great desire was to erase any fear that they were going to be abandoned. Within the context of promising his abiding presence Jesus commanded their attention with one of his mind-boggling and emotionally-penetrating statements. "He who believes in Me, the works that I do shall he do also; and greater works than these shall he do" (v. 12). This is so staggering that we want to reject it. How can we with our human frailty and human inefficiency do anything greater than God? Check closely the word *greater*. Jesus did not infer that we would outdo God. The word *greater* means greater in quantity. Jesus is saying you will be able to do more than I have done, and he was speaking about the amount of his actions through the course of history as compared to his earthly ministry. Careful here. They will still be his works. We only come in at his invitation.

When God chose to send Jesus Christ into the world he chose also to impose limits upon him. Patient now, stay with me. Jesus ministered in a specific land area that was comparatively small in size. He worked among a numerically limited group. He spoke primarily in one language. All of this was necessary to reveal God's activity in a local area and is by no means meant to minimize the ministry of Christ. Throughout his life Jesus periodically gave hints that his work would expand and increase. No fewer than three parables testify to this expectation. He spoke of a mustard seed, and he compared its size to the tree produced by the seed (Matt. 13:31-32). The story of spontaneous growth in the kingdom carried the theme that the kingdom would persistently increase (Mark 4:26-29). Finally, he gave us the picture of yeast spreading through dough to indicate that his ministry would likewise spread for the goodness of the whole world (Matt. 13:33).

A quick survey of the history of missions and Christian expansion in the world exemplifies the greatness of what has been going on through his believers and followers. Today the gospel has been preached in all continents. Legions of institutions for healing have been founded through the Christian cause. Numerous schools and centers for learning have been established out of someone's commitment to Christ.

Still, so much is possible in the area of great works for him. We live in an unprecedented era of mass communications. We can travel farther with the gospel than any previous generation. There are more means of healing through hospitals, doctors, nurses, and medical technicians than ever before. Greater works are being done than in the time He chose to limit himself in the Judean area.

Now let's bring this down to where you and I live. It is possible for each of us to do greater works for him! Yes, we have access to more people than the believers of his time. Granted, there are excellent training opportunities existing for us. True, we have outlined areas of ministry and defined needs. Even so, before we can do these greater works we have to come to grips with what God is doing now in us as individuals. The individual Christian, you and I, must always march under the banner of possibility. That which is possible for the church will become reality only when the individual Christian comes to grips with what God is doing or trying to do in his personal life.

Whatever God Is Doing in You Requires Your Faith in Him

"He who believes in Me" (John 14:12). The condition required for producing greater works is the basic experience of faith. Whatever God is doing in you requires faith.

There is no doubt that God was active in the life of Abraham, who was willing to faith God and willing to expose himself to a new land. He risked failure and the possibility of being wrong. His chosen way was to cut off the security he had at home and march behind a big question mark, moving from the relative safety of his earlier life toward the unknown land.

Exactly the opposite from Abraham, we attempt to build many securities into our life-styles. I vividly remember an elderly gentleman in my hometown who owned an old grocery store. Almost daily he had to do something to prop up his old store. The building was literally rotting down, and instead of doing major repairs he would nail on another board, jack up a corner, or prop up one of its leaning sides.

Many lives are lived in the same way. We keep trying to prop up ourselves on the leaning side. But there are certain parts of life that can only be dealt with by faith in God. There are times when our ability to handle a certain task is questioned, and all we can do is to faith God. All parents experience frustrations in the attempt to correct or redirect the behavior of a child, and "authorities" in the area of childhood education and pediatrics often seem inadequate and irrelevant. We can faith God for answers.

Sometimes even on clear and bright days no sunshine breaks into any part of our lives. We must faith the light of Jesus Christ which comes to us in faith. Life, if lived at all in the world, will include broken relationships. Sometimes we wonder what has been said or done to sever a tie with someone we love. No recourse other than faith in God is available. Sometimes feelings literally lord it over our existence and master us. We must faith God to know the right decisions and choices to make. These are some of the times when God is doing some of his best work in us. All of these stated conditions are possible occasions when God may be intensely active in us.

Whatever God Is Doing in You Agrees with What He Did in and Through Jesus Christ

In the nearly two thousand years since Jesus' ministry on earth, more and more of God's workings and doings have been taking place in increasing quantity. To think that we can continue on with what God was doing in Jesus Christ is a very heavy, humbling, and staggering responsibility.

In the fall of 1966 I returned to the seminary to begin my graduate studies. Immediately I went over to visit one of my professors. As soon as I walked into his office he said, "I have been trying to call you for a week. I want you to serve as my graduate fellow." I had utmost respect and appreciation for this man and considered the students he chose to serve as his fellows to be honorable and dedicated students. I never dreamed he would ask me to work for him. Now I was faced with the opportunity and responsibility of continuing a reputation of integrity and fairness in grading as well as willingness to assist the students. It was a heavy task to assume. The sobering fact, startling reality, exciting possibility exists that God will want us to carry on what he began in Jesus Christ. This is exactly what Jesus said.

But what did God do through Jesus?

Review chapters 3 through 6 of John's Gospel, the personal section that narrates the activity of Jesus in the lives of people. Visiting with Nicodemus, the caring and patient Savior dialogued with a man who was agonizing over spiritual realities. We can continue this ministry. Jesus accepted the Samaritan woman, yet in firmness helped her come to grips with her own sin (ch. 4). Oh, indeed, the undertaking is awesome, to try to accept a human being as a human being and to abandon our need for judgment.

We are touched by the sensitivity of Jesus as he saw the man at the pool (ch. 5). God desires to work through us to enable us to see the hurt of people.

Jesus looked upon the multitude with compassion and awareness of their hunger (ch. 6). Our God still desires to work through us and feed the hungry.

God never intended that his service to the world end with the consummation of Jesus' ministry on earth. What we are about as individual Christians and through his church is a continuation of

the ministry of Christ. Thus we better check up. Is what is
happening in you continuing the ministry of Christ? If so, that is
what God is doing in you. When the old prophet, Elijah,
recognized that his earthly ministry was nearing its end, he asked
Elisha what he could do for him. The young prophet asked for a
double portion of the spirit of the old prophet. Elisha was saying,
"Let what happened in you continue in me." Jesus was announc-
ing that what was happening in him and through him could
continue on through his followers.

Whatever God Is Doing in You Requires Your Cooperation with Him

There is no room in the kingdom of God for solo ministries.
God works in us, but he always demands our cooperation in this
venture.

Quite often he works initially in us to bring us to the point of
our willingness to cooperate with him.

The trickster, Jacob, was allowed a nighttime wrestling match
with God before he submitted himself and became God's man.
Jonah surrendered his self-written road maps to Tarsus in the
belly of a fish and reluctantly began to join the common purpose
of God. Peter encountered several lessons on the necessity of
cooperation with Jesus. Paul maintained his honesty throughout
his writings to say that he never totally lost his struggle between
his will and the will of God. Cooperation is mandatory in finding
out what God is doing in us and through us.

General George Patton is glamorized as an American war hero.
Yet if he had developed a more cooperative spirit possibly he
would not have sat out the Normandy invasion in England. On the
other hand, the cooperative spirit of Stonewall Jackson caused
General Robert E. Lee to say, upon hearing of Jackson's mortal
wounds, "Could I have directed events, I would have chosen for
the good of the country to be disabled in your stead."[3]

What cooperative venture are you making with God? Anyone who looks at the plans he has made and seeks to carry out totally his own initiative and volition probably can spot those areas in which God is not involved. On the other hand, plans, desires and hopes submitted to God become possible cooperative ministries with God.

Whatever God Is Doing in You Will Reveal God to You More

Following Jesus' broadcasted expectation of greater works he offered an invitation, "And whatever you ask in my name, that will I do, that the Father may be glorified in the Son" (John 14:13). Whatever we ask for he will do, provided it makes the Father known more; that is to say, provided it makes the Father more present. He honors our attempts to announce his presence and make him known more. Thus, whatever he is doing in you will make him known more to you. Paul Tournier has noted that "the true meaning of religious experience does not lie in the transformation it effects in our lives, but in the fact that in it we have known God."[4]

What about your concept of God? Has it increased or developed in the last year? If so, what have been the experiences along the way that have brought you insight and new understanding? These were the times when God was really working in you.

On May 24, 1738 John Wesley went to a society meeting in Aldersgate Street in London. The leader of the meeting was reading Luther's "Preface to the Epistle to the Romans." As he read the section describing the change which God works in the heart through faith in Christ, Wesley had a significant religious experience. He said, "I felt my heart strangely warmed. I felt I did trust in Christ, Christ alone for my salvation; and an assurance was given me that He had taken away my sins, even mine and saved me from the law of sin and death."[5] By this experience Wesley came to a new understanding of the reality and relevance of God.

What is God doing in you that makes him known more to you?

Notes

1. Eric Marshall and Stewart Hample, *Children's Letters to God* (New York: An Essandess Special Edition), p. 24.

2. Carlyle Marney, *Priests to Each Other* (Valley Forge: Judson Press, 1974), p. 67.

3. Clifford Dowdey, *Lee* (New York: Little, 1965), p. 354.

4. Paul Tournier, *Reflections: On Life's Most Crucial Questions* (New York: Harper & Row, 1976), p. 108.

5. Arnold Lunn, *John Wesley* (New York: The Dial Press, 1929), p. 96.